nd gelägenheit/wie sy zů diser zyt in wä
Josen Murer/ vnd durch Christoffel
truckt/ Im M.D.LXXVI. Jar.

CONRAD GREBEL, SON OF ZURICH

GREBEL

CONRAD GREBEL
SON OF ZURICH

John L. Ruth

Commissioned by
Conrad Grebel College,
Waterloo, Ontario,
in observance of the
450th anniversary of
the Mennonites

1975

Herald Press | Scottdale, Pennsylvania
Kitchener, Ontario

Library of Congress Cataloging in Publication Data

Ruth, John L.
 Conrad Grebel, son of Zurich.

 1. Grebel, Conrad, 1498-1526. I. Title.
BX4946.G7R87 284'.3 [B] 75-8829
ISBN 0-8361-1767-0

CONRAD GREBEL, SON OF ZURICH
Library of Congress Catalog Card Number: 75-8829
International Standard Book Number: 0-8361-1767-0
Printed in the United States of America
Book designed by Jan Gleysteen

For
Henry & Susan Ruth
who taught me to seek first
the Kingdom of God

Contents

Preface

Though he died young and uncompleted, Conrad Grebel was nevertheless a father among the radical Christian "Brothers" who emerged in the Zurich of the 1520s, soon to be contemptuously dubbed with the incriminating epithet, "Anabaptists," or "Rebaptizers." Many of his spiritual descendants in America carry the name "Mennonite," after an influential writer and leader in a parallel fellowship which originated some ten years later in the Netherlands. Names are less important than influences, and the remarkable fact in regard to Conrad Grebel is that most of his ideas, which seemed so radical in the 1520s, appear to have passed into the living tradition of many Mennonite communities in America, though with a distinctly quietistic coloration. When the Brothers drew up their first list of concerns, half a year after Conrad's untimely death from the plague, the tone and teachings were close to his.

For generations Conrad was mentioned primarily in disparagement by supporters of Ulrich Zwingli's state church. In some confusion, he was even for a long time listed on an index of authors banned by the Catholic Church. But when a revival of interest in the "Anabaptist Vision" was felt in America half a century ago, the fact that a collection of Conrad's confiding letters had been preserved made a fuller biography desirable. This work was undertaken by the capable Harold S. Bender, whose 1950 biography of Grebel has recently been reprinted, and will remain the classic, dependable document in the field.

At twenty-one, a year after it was published, I bought a copy of this book and read it, finding it fascinating but too scholarly for the general reader. I also observed the author's strong favorable bias toward Grebel. Through many careful rereadings, however, I find the work authentic in its massive collection of data, and candid in its precommitments. My own account of Conrad draws its life from this more basic work, and the somewhat tentative translations of Conrad's letters (mostly in Latin) by Bender's colleague, Edward Yoder. The several volumes of source materials, of which Volume II has just appeared, of the *Quellen zur Geschichte der Täufer in der Schweiz* are also, of course, indispensable.

Conrad Grebel College, in recognition of the 450th anniversary of the founding of the Anabaptist fellowship, commissioned me to render the story in a more approachable or "popular" style. Lacking systematic preparation in Anabaptist history, I have drawn on the writings of all the familiar names in the field, who will doubtless recognize many of their own ideas. My admiration for their investigative work has grown with every page I have written, and extends both to those who defended Conrad and to some who criticized him.

This is a biography rather than a novel. Some of the conversations are imagined, and most of the quotations are paraphrases. However, I have tried to stick only to documented facts, and when I had to guess, to signal the reader that I was doing so. All the information about Conrad per se can be verified in Bender's biography or in Conrad's letters, which will make interesting reading in the forthcoming edition by Leland Harder.

I am grateful for the criticisms of my first draft by John Oyer and for the many valuable suggestions offered by Elizabeth Horsch Bender. In the limited time I had for research, the friendly assistance of N. P. Springer of the Mennonite Historical Library of Goshen, Indiana, was also most helpful.

One cannot discover the meaning of a person's acts unless one appreciates the context in several dimensions. I have therefore tried to sketch in briefly some of the economic and social milieu of Conrad Grebel's Zurich. Having revised my own understanding — and feelings — about Conrad several times in the process, I leave on record in the closing "Meditation" of the book the stance from which I have come to view my subject. I have been stirred by his fellowship.

Harleysville, Pennsylvania   *John L. Ruth*
April 19, 1974

GREBEL

An Alpine Hike

At daybreak on an August morning in 1518 four men can be seen riding out from the town of Lucerne in central Switzerland. Their horses' heads are bobbing in the direction of the legendary peak of Mt. Pilatus, which builds up first in meadows to an evergreen-covered edge, and then, after a sharp swoop, to a spectacular, barren profile of rock.

Bearing their special permission from the Town Council, these jovial comrades are on a quest piqued by the persistence of ancient tales. They wish to examine a mysterious lake lying high on the shoulder of Mt. Pilatus, in which, so the populace has always held, the body of Pontius Pilate, Christ's ambivalent judge, has lain for centuries in restless intermittent slumber. Their belief is that whenever some rash intruder disturbs, perhaps with a pebble, the smooth, dark waters of this strange sea, the green peace of the valleys below is shattered with an outburst of lightning, thunder, and the deadly Alpine hail. So serious are the fears of the Town Council in this regard that they have on record a stern prohibition of unauthorized visits to this tantalizing site.

Who are these sociable explorers, and whose idea is this excursion?

As the deer and chamois disappear before their plodding horses, or the rustic upland herdsmen peer curiously after the travelers, perhaps asking to see their official pass, we may approach and listen to their conversation. It mixes Latin with quaint Swiss German, studded with diminutives and omitted conjunctions. The apparent leader, John Zimmerman, is a well-known pastor of the city receding below them. But his companions call him by a much more stylish name, Xylotectus. It is only "Carpenter" translated from German to Greek.

The pleasant, bull-necked man of thirty-four jogging along behind, the instigator of the climb, also has two names. He grew up as Joachim von Watt, son of a merchant in the monastery town of St. Gallen, but has now developed into none other than the famous Vadian, professor and dean of the University of Vienna, Poet Laureate of the Holy Roman Empire, medical doctor, and enthusiast of geography. He has retired young from lecturing, and has returned to his hometown, where he has every expectation of being named city physician. Everything interests him, especially natural wonders and the possibility that some of his young Swiss students may some day shine brightly in the company of European humanistic scholars. One of the two companions he has brought with him from a visit in Zurich, Oswald Geisshussler, is a schoolmaster of the same idealistic, modern spirit. The travelers call him by the Latin name Myconius.

The fourth and youngest man, at twenty, is Vadian's star pupil and increasingly affectionate friend, Conrad Grebel of Zurich. Hardly anyone could add more good-humored spice to this educational outing than the temperamental young aristocrat, who does not hesitate to joke with his widely respected professor, and who, in the past few days, has been trying to act as Cupid between his teenage sister, Martha, and the burly professor who is twice her age. A young scamp of exceptional promise, in Vadian's opinion. Conrad has as yet no Latin name. Give him time, Vadian meditates admiringly, Conrad may yet be the first among the brilliant circle of Swiss men of letters. Vadian has introduced Conrad to the scholarly public as "a young man of highly respected ability and of very noble character."

Moving in for a still closer look as the party pushes on up the difficult, seldom traveled path, we see that Conrad is an intense sort of fellow. If he is dressed as he likes, he is wearing a red mantle. His dark cap slopes sharply on one side nearly to his chin, and his hair is cut an inch or two below his ears. The blouse is stylishly slashed all along the arms. The breeches look skintight, and the shoes are those of a young gallant whose family belongs to Zurich's upper crust. From his belt swings a yard-long sword in a leather sheath. But why is his hand disfigured? That must be the unwelcome result of a rumpus in which he tangled toward the end of his student days in Vienna. No wonder his father, Jacob, indignantly ordered him to leave the university with Vadian. What a nuisance, Conrad

:hinks, as he checks his hand for scars, to have meddlesome friends who write back to Zurich and color things worse than they are. True, the hand was almost half cut off, but why let the ever-worrying Grebels get so steamed up about it?

To be invited on an expedition like this with Vadian should be some reassurance, after all. Ordinary students do have a low reputation — everyone knows that. Sebastian Brant of Basel said it all 24 years ago in his famous *Ship of Fools.*° Universities often disappoint the eager parents of promising young scholars:

> When of books they should be thinking
> They go carousing, roistering, drinking. . . .
> In Leipzig students act this way,
> In Erfurt, Mainz, Vienna, ay,
> Heidelberg, Basel, anyplace,
> Returning home in sheer disgrace.
> The money's spent in idleness,
> They're glad to tend a printing press
> And, learning how to handle wine,
> They're lowly waiters many a time.
> Thus money spent to train and school
> Has often gone to rear a fool.

Vadian, preoccupied as he has been with publishing a new edition of an ancient Roman geography text, has still kept his eye on the Swiss students who have been coming to Vienna largely because of his reputation. To encourage Conrad in the pursuit of literary excellence he has paid his scholar the considerable tribute of dedicating this substantial text to him, and mentioning as well, in the introduction, several of his young Swiss colleagues. "They are destined," Vadian has written hopefully, "to bring to themselves and to their native country certain unusual distinctions in learning and culture."

But the brightest feather in the cap of Vadian's "very dear Conrad" was his being allowed to garnish the new volume with a complimentary Latin poem. After crediting his professor with great and benevolent erudition, Conrad's poem concludes that Vadian's

> gift was moved by his love of native land,
> To prove Helvetia, strong in victorious Mars,
> No less a conqueress in learned men.

To be young and Swiss and a friend of Vadian! To see ahead with the recovered classics of ancient Rome, sharing with one's learned friends all the graces of the Muse! To make Switzerland — famous since Caesar, who called it Helvetia, for the toughness of its soldiery — an equally famous mistress of the arts! Conrad's mood is heady.

What drives Professor Vadian up these slopes and ridges with his scholarly comrades? What new spirit is afloat in Europe that leads men to inquiry? Surely his researches in the writings of the classical world have spurred him to join the company of those minds which tower in art and thought above his medieval culture as the snow-hatted Alps, which can be seen from the banks of the Limmat in Zurich, outrank the humble Zurichberg and Uetliberg on either side. For centuries it has already been happening in Italy. The polished Petrarch wrote in a famous letter of a trip he had made to the top of Mt. Venteoux: "My only motive was the wish to see what so great an elevation had to offer." And what had stirred in him this wish?

> The idea took hold upon me with special force, when in reading Livy's *History of Rome* yesterday, I happened upon the place where Philip of Macedon . . . ascended Mt. Haemus in Thessaly, from whose summit he was able, it is said, to see two seas, the Adriatic and the Uxine.

And now here in Helvetia, famous for warriors but not letters, here among the cowherds and mountain meadows, a native son wishes to view another little "sea" to determine what it may be that has given it so intriguing a reputation.

The pastor, the professor, the schoolmaster, and the student are probably trading theories about what they will find, as they bump along in single file, their swords flapping against the moist flanks of the laboring horses. As educated men of the new spirit, they expect nothing magical. If they did, they would not be approaching with such resolute curiosity.

No, they seek the natural, though wonderful explanation of what has been accounted for until now by pious story. Do they know that before the Christian religion penetrated these airy passes this mountain had been sacred to the pagan Celts, and later to the Alemannians who invaded the area? And is it not likely that the later

As seen from Mt. Rigi, rugged Mount Pilatus looms high above the blue waters of Lake Lucerne. An ascent of the 7,700-foot Mount Pilatus is considered the classic of Alpine excursions.

Christian priests, despairing of keeping their mass-converted parishioners from traipsing back up to their traditional heathen rites on the mountain, began to tell them that the mysterious lake was a place of evil influence? Is that perhaps how the disreputable Pilate had his corpse consigned to the pond? If so, the result was achieved. The people feared, and they stayed away. They became Christian and the swords they wielded now served the Savior of the world.

Disappointing, isn't it, that history does not allow us to stand beside the exploring party as they dismount on the petty banks of the isolated pond, and listen to the very words of their conversation? But surely no less disappointing than it is for them to find at the end of their eager quest only an unpreposessing puddle. We may imagine Conrad playfully testing the mood of the submerged corpse with more than one splash.

Having searched out the myth of the mountain, they turn to descend toward Lucerne, lying at the tip of one arm of the Lake of the Four Forest States. Passing the summer barns of the herdsmen, with their wooden crucifixes above the door, or a substantial, tall house with a turret symbolizing the residence of an official with power to enforce state law in the rural districts, or bearded mowers scything the succulent sloping meadows in neat swathes, the travelers finally cross the wooden bridge in Lucerne. After a night of rest Pastor Xylotectus bids them farewell near his twin-towered city church, and Conrad, Vadian, and Myconius head northeast together toward Zurich and St. Gallen.

The doctor has something on his mind. He admits to Conrad that Martha Grebel has impressed him favorably. No doubt he has been prejudiced all along by his liking for Conrad, who has been jokingly nagging him on the subject. Of all his Swiss students at Vienna, Conrad has seemed most promising. To have him now as a brother-in-law would be an agreeable development. Certainly Vadian's parents, particular as they are (they had made a fuss over his taking a Latin name), could find no objection to the Grebel social standing. If the senior von Watt is a member of St. Gallen's Town Council, so is Jacob Grebel of Zurich's. To be sure, one fifth of the grown men of Zurich belong to the Large Council of 212 members, but he is also a member of the small one, the inner circle called The Fifty. And this kind of class goes back for generations in the

Grebel line. Jacob had been mayor of the whole area of Grüningen, a substantial rural district in the canton of Zurich, while Conrad was growing up. For twelve years the flags on the castle of Grüningen had waved over the heads of the Grebel family residing there as deputies of the state government, and as soon as Jacob had moved back to the city he was elected to the Small Council. A leader in one of the blue-blooded guilds, a trusted negotiator and delegate to the meetings of the Swiss Confederation, a man whose political influence is so valuable that he is offered scholarships for Conrad from three or four sources — the man has status. The question is, How liberal will he be with a dowry? And what did that ill feeling mean when Conrad took his leave from the family for the ride to Lucerne?

Myconius, the schoolmaster, knows Jacob well, and communicates easily with him. Conrad, the son, finds his relationship more tense. It is, of course, fine to have a father to whom the Emperor of the Holy Roman Empire, Maximilian, grants a generous stipend handed out in quarterly installments in one's student residence in Vienna, but money is not everything in family relationships. From Conrad's point of view, his father is much too tight in money matters, and uses them to keep his son in line. And his mother, Dorothea, daughter of an official of central Switzerland, compounds the tensions with her constant nagging. Conrad tends to enjoy life more away from home.

Now that Vadian expects to be named town physician of St. Gallen, he has decided that it is time for him to marry and establish a household. However, before committing himself, he would like to take a grand educational tour extending as far as northern Europe. But he sees no harm in asking Conrad to sound out his father on whether he is welcome to Martha's hand, and what sort of financial arrangement a son-in-law of his might expect. And as for Martha, living in an expanded monastery town only a day or two away from Zurich might not be an unwelcome prospect, not to speak of the honor of having for a husband one of Switzerland's most famous men.

As Conrad talks about his family connections in Zurich, Vadian hears names of respectability. One of the three main pastors in Zurich is a first cousin to Jacob Grebel. An uncle of his, Felix Grebel, has the noble title of Knight, given in recognition of his participation in a military crusade. Conrad's aunt, Agathe Grebel, is a nun in one of the city's two convents, and his sister Euphrosine has recently taken the veil with her Dominican aunt. Two of his father's stepbrothers are respected officials in nearby monasteries. Conrad's oldest sister, Barbara, is married and lives in the cure town of Baden, just northwest of Zurich. His younger brother, Andreas, who has been with him in Vienna, will soon be a courtier of the Emperor Maximilian. That leaves at home, besides Martha, the girl Vadian may marry, only the little brat, Dorothea.

Not a common lot, this family of Squire Jacob Grebel! It is tightly interwoven into the fabric of Zurich: commercially through the iron business, socially through the Guild "Meise," politically through membership in the Small Council, by heredity through the family income realized from feudal taxes paid to his noble ancestors' estate at Kloten, and religiously through — but then everybody in Zurich is involved from birth in Christianity. The city is built on the bones of saints. It is time we entered the Limmattown with Conrad Grebel, its brilliant young scholar.

°Sebastian Brant, *The Ship of Fools,* translated into rhyming couplets with introduction and commentary by Edwin H. Zeydel (New York: Dover Publications, 1962), pp. 24, 25.

A Christian City

Looking down from the low, wooded mountain range west of Lake Zurich, we see the forest-green water narrow into a river dividing a fortified city. Thirteen sharp-capped towers rise over the notched, curving walls, behind which the defenders of Zurich's hearths and churches may take aim at attackers, be they Austrian, Italian, French, or even fellow Swiss. At the southern edge of town a massive line of wooden piles runs through the Limmat River, protection against invasion by water, and at the other end a double line of mills, serviced by the strenuous currents of the narrowed lake, serve as a severe bottleneck. Six massive bulwarks at strategic corners or entrances, a partial moat, an outer wall, and watchmen living at each of seven gates make the city safe for Christianity.

Let us follow Conrad, Professor Vadian, and Schoolmaster Myconius through the main entrance on the western, smaller, older side of town, the Raceway Gate. With a glance to the left, where a group of young men are engaged in a shooting match just across the narrow Sihl River, hardly more than a creek, the riders guide their horses up onto the moat bridge. Conrad is respectfully recognized, along with the schoolmaster, and they pass with their famous guest into the street.

Just inside the wall, on either side a thin spire rises behind the red tile roofs of the houses lining the cobbled streets. Each marks a monastery. On the left are the sisters of the Dominicans — the Oetenbach Convent, where Conrad's aunt and sister live — and on the right the smaller monastery of the Augustinian monks. Sitting at their varied tasks behind open arches on the street floor of the houses are Zurich's craftsmen — bakers, shoemakers, tailors, ironworkers — a colorful variety, all controlled by strict guild regulations.

23

None dares try to catch the attention of passersby, since all products meet the same quality standards, and thus advertising takes unfairly from one's colleague the opportunity to sell. With a population of about 6,000, it is possible to know everyone, and the reputation of being a cheater cannot be lived down. But business is not Conrad's interest.

With his two friends, he turns toward the river, circling a curiously high-walled hill in the midst of the town, crowned with tall, flourishing linden trees, and called by the Zurichers the Lindenhof. This was the site of the Roman castle placed next to the ancient crossing of the Limmat, when the town still bore its Latin name, Turicum. Now it is a place for a casual stroll. And there, seen through the unwinding street across the bridge in the larger part of Zurich are the double Gothic spires — tallest in Zurich — of the Great Church, headquarters of Myconius' Latin school. Whose statue is that — a man sitting with a sword across his knees — high on the lower tower? Charlemagne himself? Let us imagine that Conrad asks Myconius to explain the Christian birth of Zurich, and that the learned scholar tells the story in words like these:

"Felix and Regula, a brother and sister living in Thebes in the early years of the church when the Roman emperors still persecuted the Christians, came to Helvetia with a legion of missionaries to convert our pagan fathers with miraculous witness. Their success aroused Emperor Maximian's jealousy and he sent perfidious messengers to torture them into recantation. Encouraged to perfect endurance by divine signs, the faithful couple were finally beheaded on a little island in the Limmat in Turicum. Then, wonderful to relate, they carried their severed heads up the bank to a decent burial ground, making it holy with the deposit of their bones. When years later the far-ranging Charlemagne chanced to be chasing the deer on this hill by the river, not only the hunted animals, but even his horses mysteriously stopped to bend their knees piously on this holy ground. The great Emperor then gave orders for a church to be built on the site. Later it was rebuilt into Zurich's largest edifice."

"And why does the Water Church, so much smaller, stand with its foundation in the Limmat, so close to the Great Church?"

"That was built on the spot of their execution. It happens to

Though rounded cupolas replace the steep Gothic spires from Conrad's days, the Grossmunster (Great Church), symbol of the Swiss Reformation, still dominates the Zurich scene. The events in and around it helped shape the destiny of the Swiss Brothers.

be the very place where, on a little island in the river, a pagan holy shrine had been located."

"And what about the double-spired Our Lady's Church, with its abbess and nuns, on this side of the river beside the marketplace?"

"Charlemagne's grandson founded the abbey there, and transferred to it some of the bones of Felix and Regula from the crypt of the Great Church. The nuns still live from the income of the forests given to the abbess at its founding. For years she was the owner of Zurich, until the Council maneuvered her out of most of her power."

"And the tall-steepled St. Peter's Church, also on this side?"

"This is the oldest church building in Zurich, standing as it did in the 1200s."

Conrad knows that there are two more churches in Zurich, one the tall sanctuary behind his home on New Market Street, belonging to the monastery of the Dominican monks, the "Preachers," and another just beyond the roofs of the houses facing his doorway, the home of the Franciscan Begging Friars, nicknamed the "Barefooters."

A housewife shrilly scolds a monk in the street. Another joins with equal anger.

"How long," Conrad asks sarcastically, "will the citizens of Zurich support these people who do nothing but count their rosaries and pray and walk the streets in holy robes and eat and sleep at public expense? Not that Aunt Agathe and Euphrosine don't deserve a good living."

And now they clatter across the wooden bridge toward the Town Hall on the water's edge. Perhaps Jacob Grebel is inside deliberating over a message he has been asked to carry to Lucerne or Schwyz. The power of his magistracy is starkly visible in the middle of the Limmat just beyond the Water Church. It is a solitary tower, the state prison, known as the Wellenberg — the Wave Tower. Fishermen with nets circle its stone base in their rowboats, or paddle up to the two fishing huts also in the middle of the river. A massive mill wheel on each of the two bridges pumps water to the fountains in the squares of the town up the hill. And facing each other across the dark green ripples reflecting their fluttering pennants are the leading guild houses of Zurich. Conrad is home.

As Myconius in parting turns toward the Great Church, Conrad and Vadian decide to follow him, and attend the daily mass which is now being sung by one of the 24 priests who make up the staff. They unexpectedly meet George Hedinger, the Grebels' trusted family servant, who is obviously happy to see Conrad and asks about his health during the excursion. Conrad tells George to take his and Vadian's horses home and inform Conrad's mother and sister that they will walk up to New Market Street shortly. Stiff from his ride, Conrad limps under the statue of Charlemagne with Vadian.

Once inside, they hear the Latin chant drifting over the heads of Zurich's faithful from the altar in the sculptured chancel at the other end of the nave. On the walls and overhead among the arches around the windows a crowd of saints reenact biblical stories, or endure cruel deaths from men in armor — painted there by artists in the service of the faith. Wooden statues throughout the church carry out the same theme. Candles flicker their devotions. A bell rings sharply, the congregation kneels and rises, the ancient sacrifice is happening once again on the altar, *hoc est corpus meum*, the sacred moment has passed, the communers go forward to the holy place to have the wafer placed in their sober mouths, the priests alone drink the blood of Christ, and Conrad and his professor, crossing themselves, walk out onto the Great Church Square.

"Myconius is so right," Conrad might be saying. "Zurich ought to have a preacher like the priest at the shrine of Einsiedeln."

"Any city in Switzerland," let us imagine Vadian replying, "could be proud of Ulrich Zwingli."

"I wrote to him before you came," Conrad says, "when I sent him a copy of your new book. I have never felt more proud. I, a mere student, had the privilege of presenting the work of Switzerland's greatest scholar to Switzerland's most famous preacher. With your affectionate words in the introduction and my poem printed with it!"

"You can be sure he read it, Conrad."

"Yes, and I invited him urgently to come to Zurich while you were here. I said, 'Then I shall be able for a while to regale myself with the sight of three men, Myconius, Zwingli, and Vadian,' and I told him I couldn't imagine a king who would have better company than I. To think of having him relate his studies with Erasmus at Basel, or his impressions of the battle of Marignano, or to hear his

27

arguments against the Swiss hiring themselves out as soldiers. Just you and he and Myconius and I!"

"I am happy, Conrad, to see your strong love of learning and of country. You have a good start, from your years here at the Latin school and then with Glarean in Basel. You have learned the Latin language well, and you must keep practicing it in writing to me, but you have a long way to go."

"I would have been glad to stay with you in Vienna, if you hadn't decided to come back as a doctor to St. Gallen. If my father hadn't become so agitated with my behavior I might still be there. Of course the plague scared us off, too."

"Are you still considering Italy for literary studies?"

"That's where I'd like to go, since the Italians are so far ahead of us in rhetoric. But Father prefers that I go back with Glarean, even though he has now set up a house for students in Paris. The men of Zurich have commissioned him to look out for their boys there."

"But Conrad, are you willing to settle down and keep the strict discipline Glarean demands? You know how he was in Basel — how he made you swear obedience, and be in your rooms by eight o'clock at night, with no noise or frivolous behavior."

"I can take most of that, I think, and his ridiculous temper, because underneath he's good-hearted. Up to a point. And I've never had a teacher so thorough as he. Not even you, but then you were getting your medical degree, editing the geography book, and what not."

"Erasmus himself has a high opinion of Glarean. If I were going to remain a professor, I couldn't ask for a better recommendation than the one he wrote for Glarean to the Bishop of Paris."

"Let's face it though, Vadian. Money and my father will of course decide once again where I'll go. The French King wants Swiss friends; he knows they are the best soldiers. He has plenty of gold to spread around. So, Glarean's already there with him, and my father can have French pensions anytime he reaches out his hand. That means I'll end up in Paris. Luckily for me, Glarean is an excellent teacher and a loyal Swiss. And now that he's back from Italy, where the moral looseness disgusted him in spite of its learning, he's writing poems to keep the young men of Switzerland away from the whores. He says he wants us to follow Christ and Paul, not 'the world.' "

"There, you see, is the influence of his teacher Erasmus. It's the same spirit that Zwingli caught from him. It's too bad, in a way, that you weren't a little older when you and Erasmus were both in Basel. You might have learned more from the great humanist himself."

"Yes, Erasmus is stable in spite of his learning and his fame. He laughs at the stupidities of the church, like most of the humanists, but he doesn't go along with heretics who threaten it, like Professor Luther of Saxony."

"How is your health, Conrad? Are your feet still so sore?"

"Yes, and now my back is too. There's a big inflamed spot on it. Can't you prescribe something for me before you leave for St. Gallen?"

"You certainly put up with a lot of grief from those swollen joints. I wish medicine could do something for you."

"Sometimes, Vadian — soon to be my brother-in-law, I hope — I have a feeling of doom or tragedy. I don't expect to live out a normal life. But when I'm with you, or the girls, or reading the glorious classics, I am happy. I'll miss you in Paris."

"It will seem like an age while you are away. Write to me often, Conrad. I'll encourage you."

"I'll count on it. And if the plague threatens us in Paris as it did in Vienna, I'll either come back to Zurich or head for Italy."

And now, as the two friends come to the door of Conrad's home, "Tower on the Brook," not far inside the New Market Gate, we lose sight of them for a month. But we are certain Vadian leaves careful instructions with Conrad about placing his request for Martha's hand before Father Jacob. We do learn that Conrad's parents, worried about his health, pack him off up the Limmat toward Baden, the home of his oldest sister, Barbara, married to Leonhart Karli, and a mecca for people who are sick and those who imagine they are. In its famous indoor spas old and young, married and single, male and female, lounge for their health, even if they have to descend the stone steps into the waters on crutches.

This is the second time Conrad has taken the cure since he came back from Vienna. That, and the shooting contests such as the famous one held on the Schutzenhof just outside Zurich walls in September, are Switzerland's favorite recreations. But though skill in sharpshooting and pride of Swiss character might ward off foreign invaders, the baths are not always a good protection against disease. Conrad's inflamed back breaks open in an abscess on his way back to Zurich, leaving him in such misery that he can do nothing but stay in the house.

There he thinks of the books he and Vadian left back in Vienna when they rushed off before the onslaught of the plague. He wonders if the dreaded epidemic will visit Zurich too. Jacob tells his son that the money has come through from the French legate, a juicy three-year scholarship from Francis I, and Conrad can take the first installment with him to Paris. But Conrad feels uneasy about it all. There is talk in Zurich that Jacob is too quick to take money from foreigners. The Pope, the Emperor in Vienna, and the King of France, all want the fearless Swiss for allies, and before one knows it, he is entangled in secret agreements that threaten the peace of Zurich. Other states in the Swiss Confederation, such as Lucerne, Uri, or Schwyz, lean toward the French. They need the income Francis is all too willing to pay to the unemployed mercenaries for serving in his military campaigns. But Zurich has always hewed its own path, even to the point of fighting the rest of the Confederation.

Conrad is troubled by a suspicion that his father is not keeping his loyalties pure. But Jacob overcomes his son's reluctance by reminding Conrad that he, as a student, is not now a citizen of Zurich, and that it is he who will actually receive the money. There is no law about that. Everybody does it, including Felix, son of John Mantz, clergyman in the Great Church. Even the man whom Myconius has been talking up as a possible new People's Priest in Zurich, Ulrich Zwingli of Einsiedeln, accepts a pension from the Pope. Jacob heard him preach last Pentecost when he and 1,500 men of Zurich made the traditional pilgrimage to bow before the famous image of Mary. Conrad and his father are united in their admiration of this bright star of learning and faith.

One matter strikes Jacob as a little doubtful. Is Vadian really serious concerning Martha? If so, why would such a great man convey his wishes through a mere twenty-year-old student? Is Conrad exaggerating his interest? And as to a dowry, Jacob is not sure he can measure up to Vadian's hopes. So many assignments have sent him around the Swiss countryside on political errands that his iron business has suffered. Not that he minds serving Zurich as a trusted negotiator, but it is hard on the family finances. So he tells Conrad to make it clear to Vadian, when he writes, that even if they can not agree on a settlement that would make him Vadian's father-in-law, he hopes to remain the best of friends in all other matters with so accomplished a man.

When, on the last Sunday in September, Conrad does sit down to write, he first tells Vadian of his plans for school. His father and he have decided that he will leave next Thursday for Paris to study with Glarean, his old teacher in Basel. "Polite letters" will be his subject. Then the news Vadian has been waiting for. "I have tried to carry out your wishes with Father," Conrad writes. "He thinks you might be jesting, so great a man as you are, since you submitted your request through someone like me, with so little standing and influence. With your noble birth and brilliant education, moreover, he fears your expectations of a dowry may be more than he can meet. Also, he has heard that you may be considering the daughter of a wealthier family. But if it is Martha you want after all, he wishes her to be yours, as he is yours."

Whomever Vadian marries, Conrad wishes them well, and sends greetings to all the family members he met when visiting Vadian's home on the way back from Vienna, as well as the servants. And finally he reminds Vadian, "I do beg you, when you get back to Vienna, to see that my books and things are shipped home. Everybody in my house sends greetings."

Conrad finally leaves Zurich on the last day of September with two other young men, bound with him for Paris, and the servant George Hedinger. They ride out on the longest street in Zurich — Lower Village Street — toward the gate, Myconius has said good-bye and told Conrad to write often. In Conrad's pocket are three recommendations to take to Glarean, one from Myconius, one from Vadian, and one from his father, Jacob. Tied to the saddle is a bundle containing several of Vadian's geography books, one of which will be a present for Glarean, and another for a famous scholar in Paris. In his purse are the golden coins of France, first installment of the scholarship. On his belt are his dagger and sword to keep off bandits, and on his face, we believe, is a smile of anticipation. As the three students and their servant ride out past the vineyards beginning at the city walls, they are three weeks from the University of Paris, on the banks of the Seine.

Newcomers in Paris & Zurich

Conrad Grebel, seeking training in eloquence of literature and spirit, arrives in Paris on October 20, 1518. As he walks into the quarters rented for the Swiss pupils of Heinrich Loriti of Glarus among the Alps, now called Glarean, he is greeted uproariously by his cousin from Zurich, Leopold Grebel. They immediately reminisce over the years they have spent together under Vadian's instruction at Vienna. Leopold, delighted to see his old friend, declares that he not only forgives Vadian for any differences they have had as teacher and pupil; he actually considers the doctor a great and learned man, and Conrad may tell him that. Conrad is pleasantly surprised with the living conditions Glarean has arranged, which include even a garden and a courtyard. The erudite, often exasperated instructor, ten years older than Conrad, welcomes him to their rooms and table, and the whole group of students, organized like a Roman senate, assigns him the complimentary Latin name of Scipio. Clearly they expect the young aristocrat to represent a superior level of wisdom.

In the next few days Conrad goes out to deliver his letter of introduction to the famous William Budé, and to present to him the geography text of Vadian. The humanist is grateful and prepares a letter to send back with George Hedinger, the servant. Glarean writes one too. Then Conrad, in fine spirits, sits down and scribbles a long epistle headed: "At Paris from my study. . . ."

His last letter to Vadian, telling the doctor his father's reactions to his request for Martha's hand, had begun, "Greeting, Eminent Sir." But now he gushes, "Greeting, my dear Vadianus. I used to be obliged to address you as 'most learned' or 'most faithful teacher,' but after you have written such a loving letter as the one you sent me just before I left home, I can't call you anything but what I have written above. And how I would like to live up to that brotherly approach of yours by advancing my education to the point where I could be a fellow philosopher with you, as you say you desire! You say you hope that one day I'll be first in eloquence among the Swiss. Well, I would like to be included in the company of famous men, but the best part of that would be the close fellowship with Vadian. You say you love me. Tell me that again in a really long letter.

"I have given your greetings to Glarean, a very fine man, and I have told him you'll do what you can for him.

"You say you have been prevented by the fates from seeking Martha's hand. I would have been so delighted if it had worked out otherwise. May you wed a charming, noble, wealthy, and thrifty bride, whoever she may be, and may you remain a friend to the Grebel family. When you go on the trip to Krakow, the scholarly journey of which you write, I will be with you in mind. Greet my friends in Vienna (which I already see is a better place than Paris for study) when you stop there. Tell the student Clivanus that if any more money comes through from my imperial stipend he can keep it himself. I'm fairly well off here.

"Enclosed you will find letters from Glarean, the glory of Switzerland, and Budé, the glory of France, both of whom have the highest opinion of you.

"Your careful instructions about taking care of myself and watching out for even a small fever certainly show the doctor in you. If George Hedinger brings this letter to you, see what you can do for his ailments. Write to me as often as possible, and not in a short letter."

And much more, in a chatty, breezy, student's Latin. Only one ominous note — that disparaging reference to the superiority of Vienna over Paris for study. Conrad has already caught from Glarean a sense of the woeful conservatism of the professors of Paris, almost none of whom have been inspired by the new humanism. Dull, long-winded lectures on theology, jealous quarrels over reputation, and bored, excitement-hungry students are what Conrad finds. If it were not for the conversational Latin around Glarean's rooming house, there would be precious little for him to learn. Budé himself does not give lectures, and the only other offering that really interests Conrad are the lectures on Latin oratory by Nicholas Beraldus, soon to leave

34

Paris. No wonder Glarean writes to Erasmus telling him that the educational situation is so ridiculous that he prefers to sit at his quarters with a learned friend and laugh at the scholars' pretentions.

Glarean would really much rather be a clergyman at the Great Church in Zurich than be stuck in this behind-the-times French university. His testy nature begins to show soon after Conrad arrives. He is the kind of man who can enjoy a practical joke, but has little relish for one played on him. He is capable of riding a horse into a roomful of deliberating men and refusing to ride away until they give him an appointment he wants, but woe to his own students when they begin to horse around!

Paris has been having trouble with its students since at least 1200. Student riots are a tradition. Conrad has no particular intention of contributing to the tensions, but one day a month or two after he has joined Glarean's student group, or bursa, his cousin Leopold invites in some members of King Francis' Royal Guard for a luncheon. These men are hearty tipplers. They repeatedly toast Conrad's health and that of his friends. Of the students present, only Conrad tries to match their drinking. Before long he begins to joke and swear blasphemously. With Glarean watching in incredulous dismay, Conrad carries on like an ancient Roman at an orgy. Glarean orders the students to carry him out. They try to lay him on a couch and he begins vomiting the wine. When he is finally sobered up, he finds that Glarean will hardly speak to him, and then only in a low, disgusted voice. Conrad decides that this man holds a mean grudge.

Then there are girls. Conrad, in his boredom and with no lack of funds, finds numerous chances for easy sex, in spite of Glarean's puritanical poems. In Zurich the young fellows find out where to find prostitutes, and it is no different in Paris.

One episode follows another. Suddenly Glarean's landlord has enough of their noise, and expels the teacher and students together. Glarean, at his wits' end, rents new quarters for them, but is soon at odds with Conrad, who finds the cold hurting his feet, as in years past. He asks Glarean several times for a fireplace, but the teacher only scolds him for being so soft. Conrad protests that there's nothing he can do about his aching joints, and Glarean says he'll look into it, but nothing happens. Finally, when they move, Conrad is

35

delighted to find a French-type fireplace in his bedroom, and he hunts up a stove to put in his study. When he and his roommates fire it up its smoke irritates the other students, who threaten to smash it.

Glarean comes in and is soon in a shouting match with Conrad. They almost come to blows, and Conrad, white with anger, swears by the "utter damnation of my soul" to get out and find a more peaceable lodging. Joined by one of his Zurich traveling mates and another student, he locates a house with steam heat, and then tells Glarean his plans. Glarean flares up and threatens to write to both Jacob Grebel and Vadian, letting them know what a wastrel their Conrad is. He even calls Conrad a robber.

Conrad considers delaying his move, but decides that the oath he has taken is so serious that he dare not renege. And even though he has attempted to apologize to Glarean, the teacher has shown only the most grudging inclination toward reconciliation. And so, on New Year's Day of 1519, a Saturday, Conrad moves out. Glarean forbids him to attend any lectures he will give, but Conrad intends to take in any public lectures on the subject of poetry anyway. "This is anything but learning," Conrad thinks. "How can I get to Pisa, or Milan, or Bologna, where there are modern scholars?"

On that very Saturday, on the banks of the distant Limmat, a startled group of clergymen and officials are listening to the high-pitched voice of Zurich's new People's Priest from the chancel of the Great Church. It is the inaugural address of Ulrich Zwingli, given on his thirty-fifth birthday, and it contains the jolting announcement that beginning tomorrow, in his first sermon, he will open the Gospel of Matthew at its first page, and preach through the book verse by verse without omitting those portions left out in the centuries-old prescribed "canonical" readings. Further, he expects to speak straight from the original Greek text, which he has studied intensively in the edition recently published by Erasmus, translating it into the Swiss German of everyday usage.

A premonition sweeps through the conservative clergymen on the 24-member staff of the Great Church. Some of them have warned the Town Council that Zwingli, famous as he might be as a preacher, has qualities that make him unpredictable. His fine singing voice, his amazing skill at playing any musical instrument he picks up, the earthy illustrations in his sermons, his strong political views — all these have been mentioned negatively. More serious, he is reported to have been sexually involved with women in his two parish experiences. This Zwingli admits candidly, excusing himself by denying relations with nuns or married women, and fairly secure in the knowledge that he is far less practiced in this sin than has come to be expected of priests in general. The diocese's Bishop, Hugo of Constance, collects four gulden a year from each priest who wishes to keep a concubine, and 1,500 babies are born in such relationships annually. Everyone in Zurich knows, for instance, that the popular young Felix Mantz is the son of one of the better known priests of the Great Church.

Zwingli was elected fairly easily to fill the vacancy that occurred in recent weeks. Myconius is delighted. Glarean sends his best wishes from Paris, with the news that his Swiss students are celebrating the election, and the alienated Conrad, living in his private quarters, writes to Myconius, "I congratulate my friend Ulrich Zwingli that he has been appointed to my native city. I congratulate my city for finding such a pastor."

Nothing like Zwingli has ever happened to Zurich before or, for that matter, to Switzerland. True, Erasmus of Rotterdam, the man Zwingli so deeply appreciates, has lived and published in Basel, but his effect on people's behavior is far different. There are no immediate political results from his ideas. Erasmus criticizes the church with sophisticated wittiness, and asserts with embarrassing candor that there is a huge gap between the Holy Scriptures and the church which claims to be based upon them. He laughs at the pilgrimages to shrines, mocks the worship of sacred relics and images, questions the belief in Purgatory, argues that unbaptized infants are not damned, and finds the idea of Christians going to war with each other ridiculous. He appeals eloquently for people to follow Christ in His lifestyle. Glarean put it well in a letter three years ago. "You taught me to know Christ," he wrote to Erasmus, "and not only to know Him, but to imitate Him, to honor Him, and to love Him." That new attitude Zwingli has learned as well.

But when Zwingli translates the ideas of Erasmus from their learned Latin into the speech of the marketplace, taverns, and Town Hall of Zurich, people take notice. For the past three years he has resolved not to step into the pulpit before applying to himself the Scriptures he preaches. He can quote all the writings of Paul by memory, and he has a knack of going devastatingly from a verse in Galatians to a hot issue in Swiss politics. One of the more educated men of Zurich, on first hearing Zwingli preach from the tenth chapter of the Gospel of John, has the physical sensation of being lifted up by his hair. The energy, the humor, the salty language, the undeniable fresh love of Christ of this brilliant, learned peasant is taking hold of Zurich. On Sundays the Great Church is jammed, and on Fridays the countryfolk hear the same biblical eloquence when Zwingli preaches at the marketplace beside Our Lady's Church.

But by no means is everyone pleased with these amazing sermons. Some are alarmed. Zwingli's criticisms are as wide-ranging as those of Erasmus. Many in the religious establishment of the city — some two hundred priests, monks, and nuns — fear that Zwingli is undermining the foundation of their economic and social position. When they complain about his reading the omitted part of‹the Scripture in the services, he replies with the authority of a scholar that these passages have been dropped only since the time of Charlemagne; the early church is more authoritative in such matters. The priests are embarrassed to find that people regard Zwingli as far more learned than they, since he is familiar with Greek, and they can only read the secondhand versions of the Bible in Latin.

Item by item, Zwingli begins to discredit the traditional but nonbiblical practices of European Christendom. The monks are horrified to hear themselves brutally referred to as disguised hogs, fattening themselves on other people's food. Church officials who should be shepherds he calls wolves. He boldly attacks the remains of the feudal system whereby churchmen own expensive properties, collecting hard-earned rents as well as income from pastorates in which they do nothing but count up their receipts. The rising businessmen in the guilds of Zurich, who are always trying to increase their power in the Town Council, find themselves in admiring agreement with these challenges to their traditional competitors, the wealthy owners of monasteries and convents. Many years ago Zurich itself was the property of the abbess of our Lady's Church. Her power is ow a shadow, though she still owns large forests. History is moving against the monks.

Ulrich Zwingli, a priest from the Toggenburger Alps, accepted the invitation to become Zurich's People's Priest in 1518. His novel idea of daily preaching directly from the Scriptures attracted hundreds of eager listeners.

Zwingli's own eyes are too weak to see the images covering the walls of the church, but he disputes their validity. People must realize that in Christ the ceremonies and physical objects involved in worship have a dangerous tendency to replace the spiritual reality they symbolize. He dares to question the meaning of the mass itself. He has no respect at all for buying indulgences — releases from certain time periods in Purgatory. He throws doubt on the practice of baptizing infants. With Erasmus, he considers the practice of war alien to the Spirit of Christ.

Here is one of the sorest spots Zwingli touches. Switzerland has been famous for many years for its invincible soldiers, and the gold they have earned has been the main source of foreign income. This is especially true of the southern mountain cantons, but in Zurich too some families rely on mercenary soldiering as a calling by which their sons can make a living, or even a noble reputation. Their daughters, if they do not find husbands among the wealthy heirs of feudal estates, can find financial security with little responsibility in the convents in the town. These aristocratic conservatives are not pleased to find Zwingli a sworn enemy to the whole system by which Swiss citizens fight for pay in the wars of foreign kings, dukes, and even the Emperor or the Pope. Earlier, Zwingli praised Swiss victories in such wars, but since 1515, when as chaplain he saw with his own eyes the carnage of the first Swiss defeat since the Middle Ages, he has condemned the whole idea of slaughter for pay.

Whether it is war or economics or ceremony, Zwingli has had firsthand experience with the abuses he condemns. In his first parish, even though the people of the town elected him, he found it necessary to pay off an elderly priest who, in spite of several other incomes from churches he did nothing for, claimed a hereditary right to income from this parish. In his next parish he saw the rich and poor come from all over Europe to prostrate themselves, little better than pagans, before the statue of Mary, which they gullibly believed had been dedicated by a miraculous visit of angels. Let the light of the gospel of Christ in to chase out the superstitious shadows! God will do His astonishing work of restoring people to truth, Zwingli believes, if the priest only lays the pure gospel before them. The divine Word is an unstoppable as the Rhine! When a seller of indulgences named Samson comes to Zurich, Zwingli hurls at him the condemnation of Scripture, and is reassured to see the civil authorities, the Town Council, banish the charlatan speedily from their borders. This group of Christian citizens is responding to the gospel!

But if Zwingli is prospering, Conrad Grebel is not. Banned from Glarean's lectures, wishing he could study in Italy, lonely for Vadian and Myconius, he chances to lunch late in January with a traveler from Switzerland who assures him that Vadian has not married another girl after all. Relieved, Conrad writes a long letter, even though Vadian has not answered the first one, to send to Switzerland with a fellow student who has been appointed to fill Zwingli's old pastorate. "With me," he confesses, "everything has been turned entirely topsy-turvy," and pours out the whole wretched tale of his quarrels with Glarean. To add to his misery, his feet are still as painful as they were in Vienna. The cold increases the agony. But Conrad admits, even though it makes him blush, that he believes he deserves his aches as the penalty for his frequent sexual adventures with Parisian women. He asks Vadian to keep this confession in confidence and to send him medical advice.

Conrad's basic request of Vadian, however, is that he consider marrying Martha. She desires Vadian, and the Grebel family would love to see her marry the man whom they consider, in refinement and learning, "easily the first among all the Swiss."

While Conrad is writing the letter someone brings the news that Emperor Maximilian has died at Vienna and that the King of France is rumored to be preparing to go to war against Zurich and other Swiss cities that have left the Holy Roman Empire. If this is true, the Swiss students will be thoroughly unpopular in Paris. The rumors continue that King Francis would like to be the next Emperor himself.

Having written down all this very latest news, and his thoughts, Conrad begs his "most highly cherished teacher" to reply to his two letters "as soon as you can." Then he dashes off a shorter letter to Myconius, to be sent with the same carrier, asking him not to let Glarean ruin their friendship by the one-sided account of their quarrels he has been writing to friends in Zurich.

It is months before Myconius replies, and Vadian, off on a scientific trip taking him east through Krakow and Bohemia, doesn't get around to writing until Conrad has been gone a year. But long before that Conrad, in his loneliness, has gotten into serious trouble. Glarean writes to a friend that his students are going to be the death of him yet. Some have been unfortunate enough to have been involved in fight in which two Frenchmen were killed. Conrad calls the hostile Parisians "bandits." In another letter to Myconius, Conrad writes, "We can't even carry out our religious duties by going to church, nor are we able to go out on business errands without being attacked. They even invade our homes."

Deeply concerned for his bodily safety, Conrad flees the city temporarily, but returns soon with the hope of going to the royal court with some other students to reach an understanding with the King. In June he writes to Myconius, hinting at his "enormous misfortunes, my distressed mind, and inextricable state of affairs. I don't know which way to turn." He refers to Paris as "that sink of bandits and of filth."

If Conrad could only know that on the fifth of July, in a preliminary ceremony witnessed by the Grebel and von Watt families, Vadian was actually taking Martha's hand in marriage, he would be comforted. Instead, he is miserably wishing he could be elsewhere, spending his time under good instruction, learning to master "eloquence." He is so unhappy that when a messenger brings him a letter from Myconius he literally jumps for joy.

And now Paris, Zurich, and St. Gallen are paid a stunningly disastrous visit by the dread plague. Conrad and his terrified friends immediately move to the countryside, not to return for six months. If they were to return too soon, they might well join the 30,000 who perish in this wave of incredible misery. Vadian, town doctor though he is, takes his bride and hurries to Wadenswil on Lake Zurich, where Martha has a friendly uncle. They also wait half a year to return, and in the unexpected leisure Vadian finally gets around to writing Conrad a letter.

As for Ulrich Zwingli, the sensational preacher of Zurich, the outbreak of the plague finds him relaxing in a health resort. As People's Priest he has no choice but to go back into his city, and there he is struck down to lie for weeks at death's door. The best doctor that can be found prescribes numerous medicines, which Zwingli dutifully swallows. One of the older, more conservative priests on his staff, Canon Hoffman, visits him, hoping that he will confess the error of his critical sermons, now that death threatens. But Zwingli's rugged constitution holds in the long struggle, and by November it is clear that the People's Priest is recovering. In the depths of his soul he discovers a new yieldedness to the will of God and an uncanny sense that he is being spared for a purpose like that of Moses: to lead the Swiss into the gospel light as a modern people of God. He writes three hymns to express his passionate cry for help, the surrender of his will, and his praise for deliverance. Meanwhile, all about him in Zurich hovers the stench of overwhelming, agonizing death. One third of the populace has been killed off by the plague.

Just as Zwingli is laid low in September, an angry Jacob Grebel sits down to reprimand his son in Paris by letter. The tales of Conrad's behavior have reached him, and he is so upset by the brawl which left two men dead that he is unable to sleep and is generally out of humor. He orders Conrad to return home, and sends enough money for him to make the journey with a royal guard. He is especially distraught over the possibility that Conrad may have dishonored the family by getting into evil company again. It is bad enough to have him waste the money of the French scholarship by not studying, but to have him actually throw it away by spending it in the company of cheaters is intolerable.

But Conrad never gets the money. The messenger makes off with it and meets sudden death, probably from the plague. Even the letter does not reach Conrad until after New Year's, when he is back in Paris. But a few days after Jacob has written his letter, a messenger brings to Conrad, ten miles out of Paris in a small village, a response from Vadian at last. Before Conrad can open the letter he hears from the messenger the news of Vadian and Martha's wedding and he goes wild with happiness.

Filled with hope, he asks if his father has sent money for his return to Zurich. The answer is no. He is so depressed by his father's heartlessness that he lets out a bitter groan. Tears cover his face as he reads the wedding letter. It tells him that Jacob, although quite civil to Vadian, is disgusted with his son's behavior. The doctor wishes that Conrad would be reconciled to his teacher Glarean, and that he would reassure Jacob that his troubles are not due to his own faults.

Heartbroken, Conrad replies: "Your wedding is the only thing

43

that has happened in the past year that is gratifying to me. I beg and entreat the Almighty God Jesus Christ by all means and vows that you, your bride, and all our friends may be always happy. But I should have been there to greet you in person, and escort you in the wedding, and to present you with a wedding poem. Father should have seen to it that I had the money to come. When I read your invitation to visit you, I can do nothing more than let the tears come quietly and write you this sad letter. . . . You want me to be reconciled with Glarean. You will probably say that my old nature is controlling me here, but I'm telling you privately that that man holds a grudge for life. We have had another round of quarrels since I last wrote. . . . Write me again and let me know if Father intends to keep me here in this French exile forever. I am absolutely miserable."

When Conrad and his fellow students return to Paris in the winter, expecting the plague to subside in the cold months, he finally receives his father's letter — but unfortunately, without the money. Conrad reads the accusations and becomes indignant. He writes back and tells his father not to grieve. There is no reason for it.

To Myconius he writes, "Of the money, only the tiniest bit has been lost to cheaters. I haven't stolen anything. I haven't been a highway robber. I simply haven't done anything dishonorable. Father can sleep as soundly as he would like, as far as my reputation is concerned. I'd come home as soon as he provides me with the money for the trip, whether or not he's angry, and in spite of the plague. If I stay here I'm likely to catch the plague anyway. I'm caught. I can't make a decision either way."

Conrad wishes he could sometime do something worthwhile in the field of learning, like Myconius, who has now moved to Lucerne to be a schoolmaster there. He signs his letter, "Conrad Grebel of Zurich, a poor little miserable friend of yours."

Glarean finally admits Conrad back into his lodgings on the first day of the year, but beyond that there is no fixed educational relationship. As the last of Conrad's money runs out and he finds that his father apparently does not believe that the money for traveling sent in September never arrived, Conrad begins to reflect on the moral implications of his economic situation. Vadian, whom he respects and loves, is not writing. Glarean despises him. Myconius tells him that his father will not let him enter the house if he returns now. All the French gold he has brought from Zurich has been spent on food, clothing, and books, Conrad writes to Myconius. He is now a slave to money. Something must be wrong with the system.

Conrad himself feels innocent. But political rumors about his father trouble him continuously. In Zurich the gossip is that Jacob keeps some of the money from the scholarships he has negotiated for his son. His critics say he leans toward the French side politically, which is considered treasonous by some. Now he is planning to get another advancement of some kind for Conrad's younger brother, Andreas. Conrad regrets to see the boy learning to depend on foreign gifts, thus developing bad economic habits.

Furthermore, Conrad is uneasy about owing his loyalty, his very soul, to the French King, and the fact that he has given up his precious Swiss citizenship — "Helvetian liberty" — for this easy gold. The worry plagues him to death, he says. The more he considers the basis of the matter, the more he feels that he is being clothed and fed by funds which an autocratic king snatches away like a wolf from the mouth of the ordinary tax-paying population. And what if he someday emerges in a leadership role in Zurich and his financial records are examined? Won't this money-taking from Emperor, Pope, and King look rather promiscuous? "You may say," Conrad writes to Vadian, "that I'm making a big fuss over a little matter, and that the system we are accustomed to makes this kind of stealing almost a law. Well, if that is so, don't expect me to agree to it, and no eloquence of argument can change my opinion on this." Why should Jacob be so ready to hold out his hand for foreign stipends, and then so loath to let his son have the money?

Unhappily, Conrad writes home that he is totally without funds. But by March, when the plague has again begun to rage, he receives his father's sarcastic answer from a messenger, without a letter. Jacob says that Conrad knows where to get money, if he must have some. Conrad writes to Myconius that he certainly sees no way to get any. In fact, he is so desperate that he is going with the students who are moving to the country again — not to get away, like them, from the plague, but simply to live by their help.

By April he is sick. In desperation he sends one more letter to his father, with Glarean himself, who is taking a trip home. Meanwhile, on one of his many errands on behalf of the city of Zurich in its relations with the Swiss Confederation, Jacob is in Lucerne, where he talks things over with Myconius. At last he relents and sends enough money to release Conrad from his French imprisonment.

During this miserable interlude in Conrad's career, Zwingli's influence has continued to sweep Zurich like a fresh broom. Though he occasionally feels weak and has recurring headaches, his preaching has influenced the Council to cancel the singing of "Hail Marys" by the staff of the Great Church. The money which had paid for this service is channeled into the city hospital at the Dominican Monastery. The Council has also approved a simplifying of the traditional series of daily prayers faithfully maintained by the canons.

On the wider European scene the name of Martin Luther now runs from mouth to mouth. Last summer the Pope sent the sophisticated debater Johann Eck to subdue Luther at Leipzig, but the powerful Wittenberg professor storms on, defying the decadent, cathedral-building Pope Leo and calling for a Christianity based solely on God's free grace. In the week before Conrad leaves Paris, the alarmed Supreme Pontiff hurls forth the most famous bull ever to come from Rome: *Exsurge!* "Arise, Peter! Arise, O Lord! A wild beast has broken forth in Your dominion!" The battle line has been drawn. Luther is labeled as a heretic, and his ideas must be ruthlessly suppressed, even in Zurich, which is now passing Lutheran pamphlets from street to street. In further recognition of the new importance of books, the city has recently given the proud gift of citizenship to a newly arrived Bavarian printer, Christoph Froschauer.

But homier thoughts fill Conrad's head as he mounts his horse for the escape from Paris and the confrontation with Senator Grebel. A good mood steals over him. Two days out of the city on the road toward Switzerland, he meets Glarean coming back. Conrad laughs boisterously to hear his irascible teacher describe an accident he has just suffered with his horse. And then, with twenty largely fruitless months behind him, our penniless, discouraged scholar sets his face toward the Tower by the Brook on New Market Street, a stone's throw from the study and the pulpit of Ulrich Zwingli.

Idle Scholar, Paſsionate Lover

Eight stiff medieval "towers" command the roof line of the houses clustering on both sides of the ancient Roman road climbing up from the Limmat toward the Zurich mountainside, just a few blocks north of the dramatic twin spires of the Great Church. Four centuries before Conrad was born, a privileged noble family had erected the one farthest up the hill, just where a little bridge carried the main street, now a market area, across Wolf's Brook.

This has been the Grebel home since he was a teenage Latin pupil in the Great Church school. Those who live in these houses, one of which blocks the view toward the Great Church from the Grebels' front door, are known as leading citizens. They receive hereditary incomes from their ancestors' shares in ancient monasteries. Further, to live in the town of Zurich is to own the right to rule the peasants who live on lands that have been incorporated by the city, and who, without representation on the City Council, pay taxes that show their dependent status. One of the two top officials in the system, Marcus Roist, the mayor (or burgomaster), lives just across the square from the Grebels.

Stepping over the threshold from New Market Street into his home, Conrad meets a tearful reception from his mother, and a surprisingly mild, smiling city Councillor, ready to make peace with his son. Jacob has been carefully prepared by Myconius, it turns out, to give Conrad another chance. But his mother's tears have a reason beyond her relief at seeing Conrad again. Her second daughter, Euphrosine, next in age to Conrad and a nun at the Oetenbach Cloister across the Limmat, has just died. Conrad is immensely shocked and saddened. He was very fond of her, and respected her for taking the vows of chastity. The entire family hopes that Vadian and Martha will soon visit them to share their grief.

None of Conrad's closest friends are around to greet him, but the presence of Zwingli is some recompense. The People's Priest likes to share his studies in the Greek language with students, and there are sociable evenings in his home, where they read both classical and biblical Greek. Conrad has been studying Homer's *Iliad* and *Odyssey*. His letters to Vadian are marked with quotations from their heroic lines. But not everything is promising. Zwingli's critics accuse him of stirring up trouble. In Lucerne Jacob hears that Myconius is accused of following Zwingli's heretical — perhaps Lutheran — ideas. Zwingli himself claims that his ideas are not Lutheran, but biblical. Since Luther has now been excommunicated by the Pope, such a disclaimer is almost necessary to shield Zurich from serious threats from the loyally Catholic cantons. But Zwingli writes privately to Myconius that he is committed to carry through his plans for Christian renewal of the city, regardless of personal cost. "I believe that, as the church came into existence by blood, so it can be renewed only by blood. . . . The world will never be a friend to Christ. He sent His own as sheep among wolves." By his own reckoning Zwingli claims 2,000 of the city's inhabitants as followers of the gospel he has been preaching. Just now, he tells Myconius, they are drinking milk, but before long they'll be ready for meat.

After a few weeks Conrad sends a puzzled letter to Vadian, inquiring why he has heard only once from St. Gallen in all his time away. "I began asking myself what in the world I might have done that would have offended you," he writes. Within a day or so two letters come speeding back. In the first Vadian rebukes Conrad for his ingratitude in questioning his motives, and in the second he invites Conrad to visit him at once. Pleased, Conrad replies that he will come as soon as the rest of his personal belongings arrive. They seem to be held up at Basel, and include a book he wants to give Vadian as a wedding present, and also some things he doesn't want his father to see. Several weeks go by, during which Conrad's oldest sister and her two daughters drop by to mourn for Euphrosine. Conrad keeps writing to Basel but his baggage does not arrive. There is little to occupy him. He plays at composing Greek poetry, helps with the family iron business, and talks with his father about finding money to study in Italy. He is pleased to receive several manuscripts sent up from Lucerne by

Myconius. One of them is a pamphlet, still unpublished, by none other than Myconius' famous friend Erasmus on the teachings of Luther. Another, "The Friend of Peace," is a dialogue written by Myconius "on not going to war." This one, echoing Erasmus' and Zwingli's pacifistic teachings, strikes Conrad with its truthfulness. He regrets that Myconius wishes to have the manuscripts back almost immediately. He would like to have shared them with Vadian.

By September Conrad has still not left home. Vadian is beginning to suspect that he is intentionally avoiding a visit, and suggests that if Conrad doesn't care to see his brother-in-law, he should at least consider Martha's feelings and come for her sake. Stung, Conrad indulges in one of his typical pagan oaths: "May the gods utterly damn me if I don't long sincerely to see you yourself! It's just that it's not a matter of my own choice, The books and things did come from Basel, but just then Father was away on an errand and the work with the iron business was heavy. I hope to come just as soon as Father returns. In the meantime, here are two books as wedding gifts, one from me and one sent by our friend, Zwingli."

In these weeks Zurich is buzzing with rumors of the Pope's demands for Swiss soldiers to fight the French in northern Italy and his displeasure with the spread of Luther's ideas. He sends a legate to Zurich to demand that they burn Luther's books and to forbid printing them. The Zurich Council refuses to comply. But Jacob senses that this is a propitious moment to ask for a scholarship for Conrad to Pisa. Vadian approves of the idea and advises Conrad to write a poem addressed to the envoy. And so, trying to foster good relations with the Swiss, the papal representative hands Jacob a two-year stipend to the University of Pisa.

Apparently forgetting his earlier scruples, Conrad agrees to go, and begins preparations for the trip. He finally pays a visit to Vadian and takes time to travel down to Einsiedeln to fulfill a vow. Returning, he has less to say about the famous statue of Mary at the center of the shrine than the pleasant time he had at the home of his cousin Margareta Wirtz, where he stopped over.

In all this delaying, Conrad has time to practice writing short Greek poems — epigrams. He has the honor of showing them to Zwingli, who is gathering a circle of students around him several times a week, frequently eating a meal with them. They hear ominous rumors from Myconius that in Lucerne the enemies of the Reform suggest that both Myconius and Zwingli be burned at the stake for their heretical ideas. Myconius writes that he is frightened.

Conrad has now become something of a puzzle to his relatives. He feels morose and unstable. He worries about his health, although the only person to have died recently from the plague is Zwingli's brilliant younger brother. Further, Conrad begins to feel that he would rather travel north to Saxony than to Pisa. Is he eager to study with Luther, who is in the news now more than ever for publicly burning a papal bull? Conrad doesn't explain his plans to his puzzled brother-in-law, but he does write an introduction to a forthcoming second edition of the famous geography book Vadian has reissued for the humanists of Europe. This keeps the flame of scholarship alive, but something hidden, something he hesitates to confess, is eating at Conrad. Finally, when he hears that Vadian's father has died, he writes a long letter that begins with sympathy but ends by hinting elaborately, even tediously and in somewhat poor taste, that he is frustrated and confused by a love affair. He does not risk speaking plainly, but Vadian gets the general idea, and expresses amazement that Conrad still has not left for Pisa.

Conrad is seeing a tantalizing girl named Barbara, whose pretty eyes have totally captivated him. He dares not tell his family about her, because she has no social standing, and Jacob would be infuriated to find Conrad in love with a girl who had neither reputation nor dowry. Conrad loses his desire to go to Pisa, and begins to hang around the house, looking gloomy, wasting his time, letting his Greek studies deteriorate. He begins to consider going to Basel instead, where he and Barbara could be together, hinting to his friends that he might return to the university there.

A scholarship can be had for the asking from a French envoy who is just now in Zurich buying friends for King Francis. But Conrad tells his father that he will not accept any French gifts if Jacob is required to pledge allegiance to the King. The "liberty" of Swiss citizenship is worth more than any scholarship. Further, Conrad's uncle and one of his father's cousins, a well-known preacher in Zurich, tell him that both father and son are being talked about for accepting the scholarship to Pisa from the Pope's messenger.

Jacob feels increasing financial worries. His younger son, Andreas, has been dismissed with four hundred other courtiers from the university of Vienna by Archduke Ferdinand, and has returned to Zurich.

By March 1521 it is clear that Conrad, now twenty-three, has no intention of studying in Italy, even though he is offered still another Roman stipend. This time the envoy stipulates that Conrad will not get any money until he has actually arrived in Pisa. But Conrad, suffering again from sore feet, dreams only of Basel and undisturbed days and nights with Barbara. Crazed with love, he begins to consider leaving the Grebel household even if it means being disowned by his family.

By the end of April, Zwingli, already the People's Priest, is also elected a canon on the staff of the Great Church, which makes him a citizen of Zurich. Some older members of the organization are bitterly disappointed to see his influence growing. They frequently attempt to thwart his program. In spite of his urgent preaching against sending Swiss soldiers to foreign wars, the Council has approved the contribution of 1,500 Zurichers to the Pope to be used in defensive battle. But a week later Zurich defies the rest of the Swiss cantons by refusing to sign a treaty of alliance with the French, and passes a law forbidding any more private citizens to fight for foreign powers. This is seen as a gain for Zwingli, and it sharpens the hostility of his critics.

Conrad is too befuddled with love to pay a great deal of attention to public affairs. Aunt Agathe, the respected nun of Oetenbach, at length insists that he reveal to her what is making him so miserable and secretive. Conrad hestiates, she begs him by the memory of his sister Euphrosine, and he finally tells her about Barbara and his wish to escape the Grebel house. Agathe promises silence and approves his plans. Conrad also tells his sister Barbara. She is sympathetic, too, and tries to assist as a go-between. Even Vadian, informed by letter, helps to keep the secret. He asks Conrad why he hasn't left yet, in July, and the miserable young man who has secretly arranged to have his mistress waiting for him in Basel, replies that his father is detaining him. A horse stands ready if he has to run off without permission, and he says he is "dying of love" for Barbara.

The misery in Conrad's feet has spread to the joints of his hands

The Swiss Confederation, limited in natural resources, exported mercenary troops to feuding political and ecclesiastical rulers. The ceremonial Swiss Guard at the Vatican is today's only remnant of this old Swiss practice.

as well, even during the heat of summer. That and wrangling with his parents, who are concerned that he is neglecting his education, make him despondent. He has difficulty sleeping at night. His letters to Vadian are full of self-pity, like the ones written from Paris, although here at least his life in not in danger. He is now responsible to pay Barbara's living expenses in Basel, and he secretly looks up another representative of the Pope. In his zeal to win further Swiss support, the envoy gives Conrad a small stipend, a fact which he does not reveal to his father.

By August Conrad reaches the end of his endurance. He has a long, bitter discussion with his father, going over the grievances that have piled up between them, especially over money. Surprisingly, Jacob, ignorant of Conrad's real attraction to the city, agrees to let him go to Basel for study, and gives him a modest sum of money. Ironically, since he does not know about Barbara, he says he doesn't even mind the idea of Conrad maintaining a mistress, if he finds that necessary to satisfy his youthful lusts. Jacob does not dream that Conrad is considering marriage. And he is just as concerned as ever that Conrad make something of his studies at last, and bring credit rather than shame to the family name.

The move to Basel makes the miserable young scholar blissfully happy, for a while, though he finds himself deeply suspicious the first night he sleeps with Barbara that she might someday jilt him for another lover. If she does, he vows with his typical intensity, he'll never allow himself to fall in love again.

Conrad rents a room for himself at Andreas Cratander's house. He works in Cratander's printshop in the congenial company of an older scholar he learned to know in Vienna. They enjoy talking about the latest religious ideas and the ancient classics. The new edition of Vadian's book is one of the projects ready for proofreading. The proprietor is delighted to have such a pair of learned aristocrats in his service, though before he can get to know Conrad very well Cratander hurries off to the Frankfurt Fair to sell his books.

Soon Conrad realizes that the two small grants he has received are not enough to keep himself and Barbara in separate lodgings. Since he spends his spare time with her anyway, the logical thing would be to live together. But if the Grebel family ever heard of it, they'd explode, "He's living with a harlot, wasting his time letting his studies drift, ruining our reputation!" It is too dreary to contemplate once he has written about it to Vadian.

Replying to Conrad's description of his new situation, and knowing that his money will soon run out, Vadian advises Conrad to ask his father for more. To Vadian's amazement, Conrad replies that in order to save money he expects to leave his fine lodgings at Cratander's house and move in with Barbara, where he will have only one rent to pay. In the same breath Conrad has the gall to ask his brother-in-law to send him enough red silk for a mantle, and Conrad will pay him when he can, next year, if possible.

Before Cratander returns from the book fair, his ambivalent young proofreader is already gone. Jacob and Dorothea, grieving for the untimely death of their only other son, Andreas, have begun to worry about Conrad's health. They summon him back to Zurich to take medicinal baths. He comes, receives Zurich citizenship, and swears that his traveling days are over. All his scholarly ventures have ended in grief, and Barbara, whom he brings back to Zurich, now occupies most of his thoughts. He worries that she may someday leave him. In a letter to Vadian he jokingly calls her his "Barbarity." He is disturbed to find that the Grebel relatives are beginning to view him as a somewhat undesirable character. He doodles with Greek poems, and admits to Vadian his deplorable neglect of his educational opportunities. In his unproductive stay in the family home he finds his thirteen-year-old sister, Dorothea, beginning to get on his nerves. She even steals his clothes, he tell Vadian. Jacob himself admits that she's a naughty brat. But one of Conrad's friends from Paris, John Jacob Amman, who has now returned from study in Italy, finds Dorothea quite attractive.

Gradually Conrad, wishing he could marry Barbara but despairing of being able to arrange matters, is drawn back into the circle studying with Zwingli. Felix Mantz, a bright young student living a few doors from the Great Church, joins the group.

Zwingli's spiritual teaching fires them with patriotic zeal as they study Greek and even Hebrew with him and an older teacher. They are lifted high above the humdrum of daily business in Zurich as they begin to study the philosopher Plato in the original Greek. Zwingli knows how to extract ethical teaching from their academic readings. Through his influence Zurich passes another strong law forbidding soldiering for foreign pay. Those who oppose Zwingli on this issue begin to make veiled threats. A dishwasher from the Dominican monastery is hauled before the courts to explain statements he has made about coming to Zurich to kill the People's Priest. He may have been drunk when he said it, as he claims, but the Council senses danger, and assigns a guard for Zwingli's protection.

In the university town of Wittenberg, Luther's ally, Karlstadt, is publishing a book advocating that Christians destroy their sacred images. No one has advocated this in Zurich yet, but Zwingli's far-ranging criticisms have been awakening the minds of many citizens. His young students, especially, are eager to see the thick crust of tradition and ceremony peeled off the church. They are impulsive and impatient. Some want to act too hastily for Zwingli, but before long there will be excitement in the sanctuaries and Council Hall of Zurich, as (leading citizens) begin to break with centuries-old inherited practices.

In February 1522 Conrad decides that he must make a drastic move. After Jacob has been out of the city for eight days on one of his many political trips, his son suddenly marries Barbara, and immediately confesses to an uncle and Henry Englehart, the city minister who is Jacob's cousin. They promise to try to mollify Jacob when he returns. Conrad's mother is distraught and feels betrayed. She will not stop crying, and berates him violently. "If Father acts the same way when he gets back," Conrad scribbles to Vadian, "you have seen me around here for the last time. I would have left already, as an exile, if I had not been afraid it would break their hearts completely."

When Jacob returns the explosion is not violent enough to expel Conrad, but the miserably disappointed father sternly withholds any financial support. Not only is the noble family name sullied; the shabby wedding is a financial blow. Aristocratic sons may expect a dowry when they marry well. Barbara, on the other hand, represents a financial drain rather than an asset. Conrad's appeals are in vain. Though he complains to people that his father will give him no help, and the gossip about Jacob's money-grasping actions spreads, Conrad gets nothing of the family's income beyond what he needs to subsist on in the Grebel house — not even the large amount left over from the scholarship he had received from the French King. Eventually Conrad will have to sell his precious books, and he must keep reminding people who owe him small sums, just to get along. Barbara is perhaps already pregnant, and their financial misery intensifies.

One person who can doubtless sympathize with Conrad is Ulrich Zwingli, who is secretly courting a strikingly beautiful widow who lives with her three children a few doors from his residence near the Great Church. He will marry her shortly, but, since he is a priest, will not make the relationship public for another two years. By that time he, as well as Conrad and Zurich, will have seen astounding change. The first open break will come only a few weeks after Conrad's wedding.

inds a Cause

g the ancient ceremony of mass from
, but the crowds come not so much
sermons. His high-pitched voice is
very is so fast that one must think
knows when a startling illustration
, or town gossip will pop into the
learned a man can excite even the
rs. His peasant background strongly
his ideas range all the way back
nt, almost under the pulpit, a hard-
ear with his hand to catch every
ats, black-cowled Dominican monks,
aris and Vienna, typesetters from
ergymen in the Great Church — all

He has worked his way through
church in the Book of Acts, Paul's
r, Timothy. Then sensing a need
ne's trust in ceremony, Zwingli
Galatians. Luther too finds this a
radition. The Christian's first need
nd have faith, not perform cultic
prepare people for the good news
the Bible's teachings. When that is
verful force working in their con-
ces — the absurd discrepancies —
and the complicated church rules
w the truth people will inevitably
ion.

57

Zwingli is not afraid to use rough language. Jealous old Conrad Hoffman, an influential canon on the staff of the Great Church, can hardly bear to hear the monks and the general religious establishment criticized so colorfully. "If a wolf that eats animals is seen," Zwingli preaches angrily, "people raise a hue and cry. But nobody wants to protect us from the wolves that kill human beings." He is referring to the bishops and cardinals who play along with the policy of sending Swiss soldiers to war for money. "They certainly are right to wear red hats and cloaks, because if you shake them, gold coins fall out; if you wring them, the blood of your sons, brothers, fathers, and good friends runs out."

Aghast, Canon Hoffman complains bitterly that the pulpit ought to be kept for spiritual themes. Zwingli is destroying the common man's respect for Christianity itself, he charges, by chattering from this holy rostrum on the topics bandied about in taverns and shops. But the young men who study Greek and Hebrew with Zwingli at home are flushed with admiration and a strange happiness. Here is a man who is both patriotic and Christian, as learned as one could ever wish, who is unafraid to challenge the corrupt but entrenched authorities.

And what he finds in the Bible is almost too good to be true. Jesus Christ was a Messiah of peace and simplicity and brotherliness. We are to build our society on His words, and throw off the terrible burden of corrupted customs. The feudal taxes paid by the peasants are not based on Christ's teaching. The begemmed chalice from which the priest in his sacerdotal vestments drinks the wine at the mass is not the common brotherly cup of Christ's supper table. Who are these monks and nuns that we must support them with our labor? Who are these bishops who scheme over our heads to expand their holdings of real estate, who intimidate us with the power of the sword? Such leaders are not shepherds but wolves!

Conrad Grebel becomes one of Zwingli's most ardent admirers. In the inner circle of the Greek students he hears the preacher's latest thoughts. As a student in Paris and a confused lover in Zurich and Basel, Conrad has not found any particular direction in life. Now he feels the excitement of the gospel of Christ sweeping into Zurich life after centuries of being obscured by custom. His feet may ache as much as ever, his parents and relatives gossip around him, and lack of money hound him daily, but here is a cause — *the* Cause. Fired with indignation against the opponents of the recovery of the gospel, Conrad looks for an opportunity to join the campaign.

Now, during the season of Lent, what old Canon Hoffman has been fearing happens. A very strictly observed and important church rule is publicly broken. The talk goes round that last evening at Froschauer's printshop, after the men had put in a hard day preparing the new edition of the letters of Paul for shipment to the Frankfurt Fair, the proprietor's wife served two sausages. Fish, hauled in daily from Luke Zurich, is high-priced because of the Lenten demand. The men felt weak from labor. Zwingli was there, along with the pastor of St. Peter's Church, Leo Jud, and perhaps ten other men. Each ate a small piece, they say.

As the scandal boils, Zwingli announces that he did not eat any of the meat himself, but he does not condemn the others who broke the fast. The practices of Lent, like so many other cultic rules, do not have a specific biblical basis, he argues, leaving the Christian free to decide for himself. But the excitement refuses to die down. Certain members of the Town Council successfully demand that Froschauer and some of his men be jailed. The Bavarian printer, who was awarded citizenship in Zurich two years ago in recognition of his valuable skills, has become too careless.

The news carries swiftly to the Bishop himself, Hugo of Constance, who is alarmed. Zwingli decides to take the bull by the horns, and on March 23 preaches a sermon: "Concerning the Choice and Freedom of Foods." We are going to have to realize, he says, that the kingdom of God is not a question of food and drink. On the other hand, we should be careful not to offend people unnecessarily, if they don't understand Christian freedom at first. It is true that the rule against eating meat in Lent is not mentioned in the Bible, and we should not put up with such a rule eternally, but neither should one do anything according to one's own judgment or whim.

Bishop Hugo is far from satisfied with this middle position. Nine days after the sermon, three priests headed by Melchior Fattlin, a notorious lover of tradition, arrive in Zurich to confront Zwingli with the Bishop's displeasure. Surprised, the Reformer explains his views to the three clerics in the staff office, only to find that they

59

The printer Christopher Froschauer contributed to the events which led to Zurich's departure from Catholic tradition. Tired by strenuous efforts to complete an edition of the Pauline epistles by Easter, 1522, Froschauer and his crew broke the observance of Lent by eating sausage. He is depicted here as successful and famous.

are going to meet next with the Small Council of Zurich — without his presence. He knows well enough why the visitors have set things up this way. The most conservative part of the leadership of Zurich, people of aristocratic background who do not fear change, are concentrated among the Fifty. So Zwingli and his supporters report to the leaders of the Large Council, The Two Hundred, and demand that he be allowed to participate in the deliberations. A noisy fuss erupts, and the larger group prevails. Zwingli wins a tactical victory. He now knows where to turn among the officials to find support. The Two Hundred are his allies in the cause of the gospel.

Disappointed that he has been outmaneuvered, Fattlin has to listen to Zwingli not only plead his case before Zurich's magistrates, but also lecture the three delegates. There is no need to worry that faith will be abolished when ceremonies are, he argues. All ceremonies do is divert our attention from the invisible spiritual realities to the physical elements. When Fattlin charges that such opinions, openly taught, encourage people to ignore the laws of society, Zwingli is ready with an answer. "We have more tranquillity here in Zurich than anywhere else in Switzerland, and we thank the gospel for that!" Then taking the offensive, he tells Fattlin, "Bishop Hugo ought to instruct his priests to pay taxes like everybody else, and help to bear the public burdens. Wherever you go in Christendom people have a right to complain that they have to support lazy priests, monks, and nuns, who make no real contribution to public service." The Large Council enjoys that.

Sending the disgruntled Fattlin back to report to the Bishop, The Two Hundred reach a decision on how to deal with the sausage-eaters. They will release them from prison, but require that they go to confession and refrain from any further provocative acts, especially since the more conservative cantons of Switzerland take a dim view of tendencies toward Lutheranism. Aware of the tension in the town, they warn everyone to be cautious about letting it reach a dangerous pitch.

When Zwingli meets with his followers again there is plenty to discuss. The Two Hundred have sided with the Reformation! Zurich will gain the reputation of being an evangelical Christian city, leading the rest of Switzerland to glorious renewal! His followers believe Zwingli is right. Preach the gospel faithfully and society will come around. Conrad feels that he is on the side of unconquerable truth. The opponents of the Reform in Zurich will be overwhelmed as the kingdom of God bursts into European history again. Understandably, conservatives like old Canon Hoffman are disturbed, but they are looking backward. Hoffman is so upset by the debate in which Zwingli has bested the Bishop's messenger that he offers to debate Zwingli himself again before the Council. At the same time he issues to the clergy of the Great Church a lenghty written complaint against Zwingli's innovations. He feels that the Bishop is being left out of the matter.

Within a week the Council has to meet to hear reports of growing threats to Zwingli's safety. Rumors are spreading that the other cantons may abduct Zwingli to keep him from pushing Zurich farther from the traditional practices. One of the group who ate the sausage is awakened at night by some men rattling his door and yelling that he and Zwingli are heretics. But Zwingli proceeds to publish his sermon on fasting, even adding a section that accuses the bishops of imposing laws on the common people without consulting them. The people have suffered in silence because no one has preached the gospel to them that they are free.

All during the spring Conrad does nothing that brings him into the town records. Zwingli goes for a rest in the baths at Baden, and a letter arrives at the office of the Great Church from Bishop Hugo, admonishing them to halt the drift away from his authority. This sounds like a threat to some of Zwingli's friends, especially when they hear reports that a campaign to suppress the preacher may be in the wind. They meet in the home of Jacob Grebel, who seems to be away again on official business. Conrad and his wife, Barbara, are living there because they can afford nothing else. The group, including some of the sausage-eaters, decide to plan a kind of demonstration in support of their leader. It is a custom in Zurich to greet friends returning from the baths with a dinner of celebration and gifts. The men in the Grebel home plan to invite several hundred persons to such a party for Zwingli. When people see such a sizable turnout, they will realize that Zwingli has a strong following and will think twice about curbing him.

But when the Town Council hears of the plan it calls a meeting to find out what will happen at the gathering. When they learn that the leaders have planned an open discussion of Bishop Hugo's warning letter, they want no part of it. They know that the Bishop's representative has just returned from a talk with the Pope and this is no time to call adverse attention to Zurich by open-air demonstrations.

The Zwingli circle loses this round, but they win the next one when Zwingli's friend, Leo Jud, an ardent Reformer, is elected by the Town Council to be People's Priest at St. Peter's Church. This seems to be a favorable straw in the wind, considering that Jud was one of the sausage-eaters a month or two ago.

News of Reform drifts up from the Rhine as well. A preacher named Wilhelm Reublin draws audiences of up to 4,000 at Basel for his strident reformist preaching. In June he creates a sensation by substituting a Bible for the relics carried in a holy procession. This is too much, and in a few weeks he is heaved out of the city. Zwingli's position is more secure than that. But then he is less inclined to such radical gestures. He has a sense of how fast the town is willing to move.

Secretly married now for several months, Zwingli decides to ask an embarrassing question of Bishop Hugo in an open letter: Why should priests not be allowed to marry when the apostles in the Bible had wives? He reminds Hugo that several of the Swiss cantons now require a priest to take a mistress so that he will leave the other women of the parish alone. Ten priests sign the letter, many of whom are also secretly married.

There is no answer from the Bishop, and the attention in Zurich shifts to the question of the expensive monks and nuns. The preachers in the Dominican Monastery behind the Grebel home begin to defend their orders. They have been praying and preaching in Zurich for some three centuries. With Zwingli's influence the Town Council passes an act requiring the Dominicans to omit from their preaching all scholastic philosophy, and to preach only from the Bible. The head-reader of the monastery bitterly resigns and leaves the city. The monks appeal to the Council to forbid the open criticism they have to suffer, including things they hear that Conrad Grebel is saying. Looking into the matter, the Council calls Conrad and three of the men who had broken Lent at Froschauer's, for an explanation of their behavior. Conrad enthusiastically explains his

63

criticisms of the monks, much in the vein of Zwingli but less cautiously. One of the Councillors (whom everyone in Zurich addresses respectfully as "Milords") has had enough of this irreverence.

"The devil," he says, "has come into this very Council Hall."

"He's not only here," Conrad retorts, "but he's sitting up there among Milords. Because there's a person sitting with Milords who has so little concern for the gospel that he said it should be preached, for all he cares, at the hind end of a cow."

The silence is deafening.

"You might as well know," Conrad plunges on recklessly, "that if Milords try to keep back the progress of the gospel they will be destroyed!"

Conrad has brought shockingly into the open the Council's lack of unity on what to do about the monks. His heated challenge is gossiped about in Zurich for months. By a bare majority, the Council decides to call for an end to attacks on the religious orders. Ten days later the monks stage a debate between Zwingli and a traveling French Franciscan, who they think can defend their cause. Astonishingly, the visitor acknowledges that Zwingli has made the better case for his position. Sensing his advantage, Zwingli gets permission from the Council to preach to the nuns in the Oetenbach Cloister, where Conrad's aunt is a member. Now the control of the Dominican monks is broken, and, even though he preaches general scriptural principles rather than attacking the monastery outright in his sermons, Zwingli soon has the nuns thinking about returning to secular life, and turning the assets of their cloister over to the public treasury.

In August Zwingli is working on a book to answer the Bishop's warning letter to the Great Church. Hugo himself finally responds to the question of priests marrying by asking the governments of the Swiss cantons to help him suppress heresy, and implying that Zwingli is a Lutheran in disguise. That is enough for the leaders of Lucerne, who are already suspicious of the teaching of Myconius. A quick letter from him to Zwingli relates that he has been expelled from the city because he is considered a Lutheran.

Zwingli knows the situation is becoming touchy, but the issues are not out in the open, and his forthcoming book, which he decides to title "The Beginning and the End," is going to spell out his program from A to Z. Glad for Conrad's passionate support, and admiring his literary ability, he allows his student to compose a poem to be printed at the end of the book. A day or two after the book comes out, Zwingli writes to exiled Myconius and invites him back to Zurich. "You will be with friends of the gospel here, older men at the Great Church who go along with the Reform, and with Grebel and two of his classmates, the most excellent and learned younger fellows who are studying Greek and Hebrew with me and another teacher."

Zwingli's book begins to influence church leaders who know Latin. It claims that Zurich is a Christian city, in which people do not need priests or a pope to relate them to God. Zwingli includes a general accounting of his preaching efforts to date, in answer to Bishop Hugo's warnings. Some surprising and controversial points are stated very clearly, such as the claim that the tithes required by state authority for the support of church institutions are not biblical, but that they should be paid anyway. All that is really needed is that the Word be preached. God's Spirit will take care of the rest. And finally, just after the "Amen," appears a stylish Latin poem crafted according to an intricate classical model by the son of a Zurich city councillor, Conrad Grebel. It sums up Zwingli's teaching and shapes it into a passionately indignant challenge:

> Now let those bishops ramp and rage together —
> Those "bishops" who in fact are hungry wolves —
> Because the truth, resurgent in the world,
> Is blazing in its ancient gospel light.
> And more, the bold and subtle Lucifers
> Are all sent packing by divine command.
> Still more (a truthful prophet, I shall speak),
> Because their empire and their tyranny,
> Their holy bans, rules, priesthood bought for gold,
> Rank murders of the honest populace,
> Imposing line of sacred merchandise,
> Pronouncements, thunderings, superstitions —
> All are led captive by the gospel Word,
> And will be led in strictest triumph with
> Those "bishops" who in fact are hungry wolves:
> Now let those bishops ramp and rage together.

Conrad signs his name at the end: "In gratitude for the recovered gospel." Zwingli's sympathizers are delighted to see the
well-known family name with the poem. They note with satisfaction
that the Reformer has followers among Zurich's noble families. One
man writes after reading the book that it gives him great joy to learn
that Conrad Grebel has developed into an outstanding promoter of
the gospel.

From now on there is only one direction possible — forward
with Christ. The momentum can be felt in Zwingli's next published sermon:

> The Word of God is sure; it cannot err. It is clear and does not let it-
> self wander into the shadows. It opens itself up and shines into the
> human soul with grace and salvation. It brings the soul to trust in
> God; it humbles the soul so that it throws itself upon God.

These words he preaches to the nuns, who are now asking how they
can lay aside their religious habits.

Every few weeks now, the fallout of these sermons is evident
in a new way. In the village of Hongg, just north of Zurich, the
fiery pastor Simon Stumpff has convinced some of his parishioners
that, as Zwingli says, state-collected tithes are not biblical, and thus
(although Zwingli does not agree on this point) the peasants need
not pay them. It is especially galling to be required to support a
priest who will not preach the gospel and support the Reform. Zurich's apprehensive officials call in the most vocal opponent of the
tithes and jails him. At a hearing the man objects to what the head of
his local monastery does with his money. The abbott is too Catholic
for his taste.

Then there is Wilhelm Reublin, who has just immigrated from
Basel. He breaks the fast laws in public, and when called in, says
he has done it for reasons of health. Fair enough, says the Council, but keep it private if that is the reason. Another issue that
stirs up Zurich is the old question of accepting pensions from foreign governments. Zwingli is pleased to see the Council absolutely
forbid both this and mercenary soldiering.

Keeping on top of all these concerns makes Zwingli feel over-
loaded. He resigns as People's Priest and the Council reappoints him
simply as a preacher. The general impression is that someone else

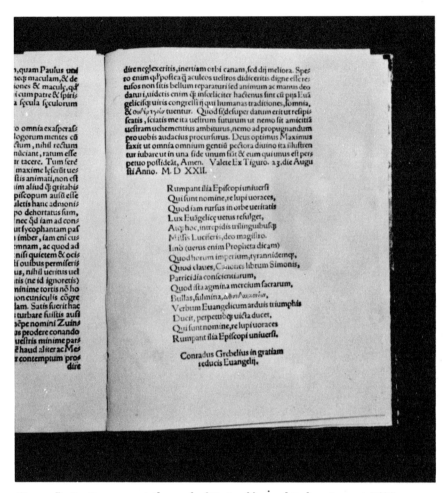

Conrad's Latin poem at the end of Zwingli's Architeles, August 1522.

will get his former position, but as the weeks roll by no one is appointed. No one will ever be. By never getting around to the matter, the organization of the Great Church shows that it doesn't need a priest. This gets Zwingli off the hook — he no longer needs to preside over the mass. It is clear from his preaching that he is dissatisfied with the old ceremony, and his pupil Conrad now says the mass crucifies Christ afresh. Vadian even hears a rumor that Zwingli plans to attack the mass in writing and asks Conrad if this is true. "Not that I know of," replies Conrad, "and I ought to know, because I'm so close to him here in Zurich that I can practically touch him by reaching out my hand from our house."

A son is born to Conrad and Barbara, and they name him Theophil — lover of God — in the spirit of the new faith. He tells Vadian that he is burdened with debt, and he feels he is living in a kind of exile with his little family. He asks Vadian to collect every penny that a man near St. Gallen owes Conrad for shipping him some books. "Otherwise," he writes, "it is all over with me." But suddenly he changes the subject in an outburst of indignation. Vadian has told him that the head of the monastery in St. Gallen is trying to hinder the budding Reformation there. The cautious Vadian does not feel that he himself can do much about the situation, and Zwingli, Conrad muses, is too busy.

"I'd take on those blasphemers myself," Conrad threatens, "if I only knew the Scriptures better. Oh my dear Vadian, if you only knew what a burning passion I feel to attack this kind of wolves, to the point that I don't even hold my life dear if I could get the chance to condemn these men publicly! I wish everybody would pray for me, that I would be able to get into this work, and I mean in earnest. I won't say more about it, because wagonloads of words would not be adequate to express how strongly I feel. Sometime I'll prove that I'm serious about this by doing something about it." Conrad closes his letter with a new note for him. He greets "the entire church" in St. Gallen, "which belongs to Christ. Good-bye, Vadian, evangelically."

On December 1, 1522, the Council decides to stabilize the fermenting situation, and orders the nuns of Oetenbach to stay in their cloister at least until Pentecost. There is a great to-do in the debate, and later that day, Conrad, in spite of severe headache, writes a short letter to let Vadian know what has happened, and to tell him that his thirteen-year-old sister, Dorothea, is requested by her parents to come home. When he thinks of the pastor in St. Gallen, Benedict Burgauer, he tells Vadian to excuse him for not sending a letter. "If I have been able to get free enough of my engagements to write the pastor, let this right hand of mine, O Jupiter, drop off." (Zwingli writes much the same way, but he says, "By Hercules.") "However," Conrad jokes, alluding in the words of the Apostle Paul to the priest's recent marriage, "I desire that he be well and without reproach, this husband of one wife."

Zwingli, to whom Conrad is very close just now, is pleased with the support he is getting from key people in Zurich. He writes to Vadian that, though there are serious dangers, the work is going along nicely, if slowly. He compliments both Conrad and Jacob, his father, telling Vadian of their diligence. But the news from the other cantons is ominous — they wish to roll back Zwingli's changes — and in Zurich itself threats are made against Zwingli's life. When one of the other preachers, Leo Jud, tries to present a sermon in one of the monasteries, a monk keeps interrupting, and Jud barely gets away without a fight. Such things keep Zwingli so preoccupied that he asks Conrad to write to Vadian about securing a Reform-minded pastor to fill a vacancy that has just opened at Winterthur.

Happy to do "this incorruptible man" a favor, Conrad lets Vadian know in passing that he hasn't one penny to rub against another. And he doesn't know what to make of his mother. "She's ungodly toward me, and to my wife she's downright rabid. I actually fear for her salvation unless she puts on Christ and becomes a new creature born again by the divine Spirit. And now the time is drawing close when most people eat the body of Christ unworthily, if they haven't forgiven the trespasses of others in a brotherly spirit." Then Conrad bursts into a prayer, "O Christ, send Vadian or someone like him to teach her from your truth to give up such ungodliness, and to teach me patience."

Four days after writing this letter, Conrad hears of a momentous step taken by the Zurich City Council. Invitations have been sent all over the country, to every priest in the canton of Zurich, to the Bishop of Constance and other leaders, for a full-scale discussion in the Town Hall on the questions raised by the Reformation. Zwingli will expose his ideas to the assembled delegates, who may then offer criticism, but only on scriptural grounds. No one will be allowed to appeal to tradition. The Reformer is hard at work on a list of 67 theses on topics such as faith, the mass, saints, good works, fasting, pilgrimages, images, purgatory, and the church as secular power. After the discussions, the Town Council will decide what course of action to take in dealing with these issues in the unfolding life of the city.

That, replies the Bishop indignantly, is beyond the proper powers of the Council. In matters of faith the church is its own authority. That is why we have bishops and a Pope. He refuses to honor the out-of-order assembly with his presence, but sends an important aide, Dr. Faber, to observe.

As Conrad enters the Town Hall on the morning of January 29, 1523, excitement grips the city. Some 600 men have filled the chamber. Faber can be recognized by his red hat. He carries two large Bibles — one in Greek, the other in Hebrew. After Conrad's neighbor, Burgomaster Marcus Roist, opens the meeting. Zwingli offers anyone present a chance to prove his 67 theses unscriptural. Everyone is silent. Vadian looks around calmly. Finally a Reform-minded village pastor challenges Faber to respond. The Bishop's envoy replies, "We can't discuss the kind of issues my dear brother Zwingli raises in this kind of a meeting. That is only for a general council of the church, or universities like Paris and Louvain. Furthermore, a legitimate council has been called for Nuremberg."

"But why should we wait for that?" Zwingli asks. "Aren't there enough people here, and educated people, too, to decide about these customs? You men of Zurich can settle this without councils and bishops. God gives you this freedom."

Only reluctantly is Dr. Faber drawn into the inconclusive debates on tradition, celibacy, or the saints. By noon of the second day only a few of Zwingli's theses have been worked over. But it is clear to the Councillors that Zwingli is winning the debate, and Zurich is going to keep the Reform developing. Faber protests the unfairness of having him answer 67 theses that have barely been printed in time for the disputation. He particularly wants to discuss the thesis on whether the mass is an offering — a sacrifice — or just a memorial. But no agreement emerges. Zwingli closes the discussion by saying that in secular questions the decisions need to be made by the

Councillors, but in spiritual matters only the Scripture, through which the Spirit speaks, may be the judge. He advises everyone at the disputation to read the Bible, either in Latin or German. At that a village pastor calls out that he does not have enough money to buy a Bible. The Council deliberates and resolves that, since no one has refuted Zwingli, he is to proceed as he has been doing until he is instructed better. Dr. Faber heads back toward Constance with bad news for Bishop Hugo, and Zwingli's circle of friends is jubilant. Zurich is now being reformed — with the official stamp of the Council!

As Conrad walks back with Vadian to the Tower by the Brook on Newmarket Street, where he and Barbara still live reluctantly with his parents, it does not occur to him that in less than a year he will agree with Dr. Faber — the Zurich Council's claim of authority to make decisions for the Christian church in the canton is open to question. But for now — what a victory!

The Council & the Gospel

As the lime trees on Zurich's ancient Lindenhof hill begin to flaunt their silvery-green foliage, Conrad and Barbara Grebel are expecting their second child. Their homelife is difficult. Gray-haired Senator Jacob offers no financial help. Conrad feels forced to turn to others for aid. His health remains poor, and he has a premonition of death.

Yet, when he thinks of the new developments in Zurich, he is optimistic. "All goes well," he writes Vadian in June. "The nuns may now leave the cloister at Oetenbach, if they wish, taking whatever property they brought along when they came. Those who want to stay will have to continue wearing their habits, so that they won't offend 'the weak' (or rather, the ones that rebel against the gospel). This has been decided by The Two Hundred." But Conrad is disturbed by something he has heard from St. Gallen. The pastor there, Benedict Burgauer, has been criticizing the more outspoken friends of Reform in Vadian's city. "I always was afraid," Conrad comments to Vadian, "that people like your pastor would put their sophistication ahead of their faith. If he insists on backsliding to the old pagan practices, I can only hope that someone else will fill the pastorate in St. Gallen."

This is a strong language for the ears of a moderate man like Vadian. Conrad is so quick to call an abuse an "abomination," a friar a "wolf," or a harsh government official a "Turk." Now he speaks of Vadian's pastor as turning back to the "vomit" of the traditional teachings.

When Burgauer hears this, the irritated pastor replies reproachfully to Conrad: "If I did not believe in returning good for evil, as Paul teaches, I wouldn't write an iota to my Conrad. I have good reason to be annoyed with you for making yourself believe that I have stopped supporting the gospel, and so ought to be replaced in the ministry. What I have done is to deal sternly with some people who were using our new liberty as an excuse to indulge their flesh: they were crowing that we shouldn't pray for the dead, that we ought to get rid of the mass, that babies who have no faith of their own shouldn't be baptized, and so on. I denounced these people as false and divisive."

It is quite obvious that Benedict has been polarized, and he hints that Conrad is guilty of "impudence" for questioning his motives. "Why, these babbling good-for-nothings attack the priests, they destroy customs, they get drunk, and then they have the gall to defame the priests, calling them robbers. This is what these Christians call gospel. Now you see what motivated me, Conrad. You need to learn some basic lessons from Scripture, instead of being so carnally envious." After all that, Pastor Burgauer addresses his letter, "To the very upright Conrad Grebel of Zurich, a most affectionate brother in Christ." This is typical of reactions to Conrad. His friends love and admire him, but they think he is too impetuous, too critical, too angry.

Two of the hottest issues in Zurich this summer are the legally enforced tithes paid by the peasants to support the various church organizations, and the ceremony of the mass. Now that Zwingli has preached that these obligatory tithes are not scripturally commanded, the peasants in half a dozen villages are balking at bringing them in. How can something that the Bible calls voluntary be enforced by the government? they ask. And why, after providing this way for the support of the clergy, must they pay extra fees for weddings, baptisms, funerals, and who knows what else?

The Council calls for hearings. Conrad watches eagerly for the outcome, wholeheartedly sympathizing with the peasants. Though he himself, as an aristocrat, does not share their tax burden, his poverty helps to sharpen his feelings for the underdog. When the Council decides that the tithes must remain for the sake of order, Conrad is jolted. "Our city fathers," he writes angrily to Vadian, "are behaving like tyrants." Zwingli is calling Zurich a Christian city, but this matter of the tithes, Conrad says, is handled as it would be by "people of the world."

Zwingli himself speaks more cautiously. He now feels that his role is to orchestrate the Reformation with discretion, moving forward in the gospel only as fast as sufficient support grows in the minds of the people who hear his sermons. But if individuals launch their own ill-timed reforms, the whole movement will be considered eccentric. A day or two after the Council insists on the tithes, Zwingli preaches a powerful sermon on the question. "We have to see the difference between the perfect righteousness of God and the flawed goodness of man at his best," he argues. "Because of man's imperfection, we need magistrates, and they are given control by God over our outward behavior. In the outward realm, then, we must obey them. In the inner, spiritual realm, they have to submit their decisions to the Word of God. Even though the Word does not require us to pay the tithes, we should pay them when the government requires them, because this is an outward matter. Those who refuse to pay deserve to be punished, because those who withstand the law of the magistrates resist God's law."

On the other hand, Zwingli has no intention of letting the dozens of clergymen in Zurich go on making an easy living chanting repetitive unnecessary prayers. The money from the tithes should be used for a staff one tenth the size of the present one, and what is thus saved should go into Zwingli's pet project, a college where the Scriptures can be studied. This will be headquartered in the Great Church itself, where a circle of young men, including Conrad Grebel, are already deep into the Greek and Hebrew Scriptures.

The staff of the Great Church is becoming uncomfortable, as Zwingli initiates an investigation of complaints about their behavior. The question of the mass heats up when one of the priests, Dr. Lawrence, goes to the neighboring fishing village of Zollikon to preach. There on the hill overlooking Lake Zurich two brothers, one of whom had been called before the Council with Conrad over the criticism of the monks, take the learned priest to task. Jacob Hottinger tells the doctor that it cannot be proved from Scripture that the bread is the actual physical body of Christ, and that as a priest he should give both bread and wine to the congregation not reserve the wine for himself, as has been done for centuries.

"Ulrich Zwingli is a clever, learned man," the priest replies, "and he is not able to bring about the change. What can I do about it, then?"

Hottinger, uneducated as he is, barks back: "If you can't do it, let me!"

Irreverence like this is alarming. "We priests in the city really do not know whether we are safe," writes one member of the Great Church staff. The average person no longer respects the mass because it is being called a fraud in the pulpits.

Meanwhile, Zwingli has an important conversation with a wandering scholar from Holland, Hinne Rode. This man has been dismissed from his position in a school at home because of his "Lutheran" leanings. His special interest is the meaning of the Lord's Supper. What he says fascinates Zwingli. Christ's words, "This is my body," the Dutchman explains, must be interpreted carefully. The meaning is clearer if we quote it thus: "This *means* or *signifies* my body." As Zwingli passes this idea on to his followers, they begin to see the Lord's Supper not as a sacrifice, repeated endlessly, but a memorial — a reminder. Now the young evangelicals of Zurich lose all interest in the mass. It is a hindrance, an abomination, and some even begin to say it is from the devil. In August Zwingli publishes suggestions for revising the mass to make it less offensive.

Conrad agrees that "the bread is nothing else but bread," but as he studies the Scriptures more closely he begins to see that it is a bread of brotherhood as well as of remembrance. When he writes to Vadian he slips into scriptural phrases that show that he has begun an intense searching of the Bible. Conrad and Barbara name their second child Joshua, although the Grebel relatives none too delicately object to it. Conrad considers their tastes worldly. He proudly spells the name out for Vadian in four different ways, showing its Hebrew and Greek forms. Since "Joshua" is a Hebrew name meaning "Jahweh is deliverance" and its Greek form is "Jesus," it is evident that Conrad has now brought his new evangelical faith into the center of his consciousness. But as to having Joshua baptized, Conrad seems never to have questioned it, even though Pastor Burgauer of St. Gallen reports objections to infant baptism there. Zwingli, with whom Conrad remains intimate, manages just this week to have the baptismal service changed from the traditional Latin into the German language.

The issue that has tongues wagging most is the question of images — painted on walls or carved from wood — in Christian worship. Zwingli has often said that they seduce the worshipers' attention from the spiritual to the worldly, and now people are calling them idols. Up in Wittenberg Luther's cohort, Karlstadt, has been condemning images for several years. On September 1 Leo Jud, pastor of St. Peter's Church in Zurich, preaches a powerful sermon calling for removing the images from the city's Christian sanctuaries. Gossip has it that Leo wants to see the images struck from the altars with an ax! In a few days torn-up pictures are found on the floor of the chancel. Then the altar itself is smashed by an unknown hand. The eternal flames in Our Lady's Church are snuffed out. At a wedding party some images are thrown from a window into the Limmat. Soon Laurenz Hochrutiner, a weaver, is named as the ringleader. He and his comrades have also been playing with holy water. To appease the growing consternation the Council locks Hochrutiner and three companions, including the controversial cobbler, Claus Hottinger, into the jail tower where they have three nights to cool their zeal.

They are no sooner released, however, than a miller just outside the city gate at the southern end of town finds them eyeing the large wooden crucifix planted there. "When are you going to get rid of your idol?" Hottinger wants to know.

"That is a matter that should be left to Milords," replies a miller.

"A good Christian would obey what Scripture commands and do away with it," says Hottinger. Then he and his friends break the crucifix and dig the base out of the ground. Hottinger says the wood will be given to the poor.

This time the reaction is more serious. Damaging churches has traditionally brought the death penalty, and Zurich contains many people, including an element in the Small Council, who want to keep the images. Even Zwingli has approved the death sentence for a man who stabbed a religious painting in a tavern, claiming that it had no special sanctity. The iconoclasts are led back to jail. A commission, including Jacob Grebel, is appointed to consider the matters of images and also the mass. What shall be the next move in the Reform? The commission is asked to report to the City Council after studying the relevant biblical passages with the three city preachers. Zwingli hopes that other cities will follow this practice of having the governing magistrates exposed to the Word of God.

Since the disputation in January has worked out so well for the orderly furtherance of the Reform, the commission feels that another one, to clarify the questions of images and the mass, would ease the tension. On October 12 the Council sends out invitations to all the clergy and important officials of the canton of Zurich, representatives from the other Swiss cantons, and three bishops. The idea is "to hold a discussion and help to make a decision from the Old and New Testaments." Jacob Grebel writes personally to his son-in-law Vadian, who is to serve as one of the chairmen of the discussion, expressing his hope that "with divine help things might find a unifying solution."

On October 25 the citizens of Zurich gather in the Great Church, under Zwingli's leadership, to call for divine guidance in the upcoming discussion. The next morning, with the three iconoclasts still sitting in the jail tower in the middle of the Limmat, some 800 men crowd into the Town Hall on the bank, just a few hundred feet downstream. Over 500 priests have come, but no bishops. The Two Hundred are ready to listen to the dialogue, chaired by Vadian of St. Gallen and Sebastian Hofmeister of Schaffhausen. Dr. Balthasar Hubmaier, a learned pastor, has come down from his congregation at Waldshut.

Zwingli begins by assuring the assembly, as he did in January, that they represent the Christian church of Zurich and as such have a right to deliberate on possible new steps, as the Scripture will teach. Because the Town Hall is too full for the people to kneel, Zwingli suggests that each one should ask God in his own heart to direct his thinking. Then the question of images is taken up. When it is suggested that they should not be removed from the churches too rapidly, since some weaker Christians need them as a crutch for their faith, Zwingli counters that they are forbidden by God, and must be eliminated. Conrad Grebel speaks up and says that if public images are to be abolished, individuals should also be forbidden to have them. By evening the chairman observes that the discussion has made two basic points: the images should be removed and the iconoclasts should be dealt with leniently.

The next day's deliberation begins with a complaint that people are saying that the mass and the monks' orders come from the devil.

Zwingli admits that he is probably to blame for such statements, because he has made general attacks on these two institutions, which certain crude people have twisted. In general, the trend throughout the day is to declare the mass unscriptural. But Conrad, who is eager to see just how serious the assembly is about carrying out the scriptural teaching, is disturbed when he finds they are about to move on to another topic — purgatory. Conrad rises to call for some specific plan whereby the priests will be instructed to stop saying the mass, now that the "church," as Zwingli has called the assembly, has determined that it is unscriptural.

Zwingli responds, "Milords will be making provision for proper action about the mass."

What follows is rather confusing, but Simon Stumpff, a radical priest from the village of Hongg, rises to disagree. "The decision has already been made by the Spirit of God."

Zwingli does not feel an important issue is at stake here. It is primarily a matter of timing. He sees no point in creating dissension now that the basic point has been gained. One step at a time.

But Conrad has something disburbing to ponder on his way back to Barbara that evening. What if the Council decides to delay giving up the mass? Does that mean the priests will have to go on chanting it even though the church has called it an abomination? And supposing the priests decide that they cannot continue in good conscience. Are they subject to the Council's command or the Word of God? As Conrad talks things over with Vadian, he begins to see Zwingli in a slightly different light. The bold, imaginative preacher of the Word can deal out criticism very colorfully, but, as one thinks about it, he is careful not to tread too hard on the Councillors' toes. He needs them on the side of the Reform. *But* — does this friendship with political power mean that the Word of God must wait until the Council is ready to have it carried out? This divine Word that Zwingli has said is as unstoppable as the Rhine? Conrad is uneasy.

The next day begins with a sermon by Zwingli. Then at Conrad's request the assembly continues its discussion of the mass. Conrad is called on to present an introductory speech, but he declines, saying he would rather hear from someone else since he is not a good speaker and has not had time to pull his thoughts to-

The debate in the Grossmunster in 1523 is often regarded as a decisive moment in Zurich's Reformation, preparing for the later emergence of the Swiss Brothers and raising the issue of the separation of church and state.

gether sufficiently. Balthasar Hubmaier helps out with some specific criticisms of unscriptural abuses in the mass. Then Conrad mentions a half-dozen traditional practices he feels are departures from the model Christ left His disciples at the last Passover. Scripture, Conrad says, calls for unleavened bread. He finds no basis for the priest placing the bread in the communicant's mouth. Evening is the biblical time for the "Supper." Zwingli feels that Conrad makes too much of minor points. It is apparent that Conrad has been reading the New Testament closely, and now wants to subject the church to it on every count, major or minor.

Zwingli's closing admonition is a warning against anyone pursuing his own private reform, as the iconoclasts have done. Then Chairman Vadian begins to summarize the three days' work, noting that it has become clear through the discussions that the Scripture does not allow the mass or images. He turns to the Council: "Here, noble lords, we refer the discussion which has now been heard to your wisdom, to consider and judge it, to submit and present the means and the way in which the Word of God will be administered and preached, and the abuses removed in your territory, without wounding the weak." Then Vadian joins with several others, just before dismissal, in asking the Council to release the three image-breakers from jail.

Conrad is thinking hard. Although he himself has not participated in the iconoclasm, it disturbs him to see the City Council deliberating a punishment for the three who had thought they were acting as Christians in clearing the church of idols. By what right do The Two Hundred, many of whom are not visibly enthusiastic about the gospel, decide this matter for the church of Christ? Conrad and his friend Felix Mantz approach Zwingli a number of times and ask him if it wouldn't be possible to elect men to the Council who will be more favorable to the Reform. Recognizing that their scheme is unrealistic, they begin to ask Zwingli if it wouldn't be better to start the church over again, dropping all support from government-collected tithes, living instead in a mutually supporting brotherhood. The circle of young evangelicals even offers to pay Zwingli's salary themselves, if he will divest himself of his state-sanctioned position.

But the preacher finds their ideas immature, unrealistic, and divisive. The last thing he wants to see is any kind of split in Zurich's society. He even has hopes of leading all Switzerland to unity in Christ. And to have these young men talk so radically at this crucial point in his plans and hopes for the Reformation is more than embarrassing; it is alarming. It seems to justify the complaints of the Catholic cantons that Zurich is coming apart at the seams with fanaticism.

A week after the disputation the Council decides on the fate of the iconoclasts. They ban Claus Hottinger from the canton for two years. They banish the weaver Laurenz Hochrutiner. Hans Ockenfuss, the tailor, is merely warned and required to pay court costs. Both Zwingli and Conrad write to Vadian asking him to do what he can in St. Gallen for Hochrutiner. "He has been punished quite severely," Zwingli admits, but it is because he has been "more outspoken." His kind of behavior must be curbed, even though he is a good man, because "there are people who will turn away from the gospel unless you give in a little to their weakness."

Conrad gives Hochrutiner a letter to take to his brother-in-law, calling the iconoclast a "brother," and begging Vadian "through Christ" to help him get a new start. "He has done nothing against divine law, or against the laws of the state, or against his neighbor," Conrad maintains. "What he did he did out of faith, and he would not have done it if Hottinger had not persuaded him that some of the leading men of the Council had advised him to go ahead. Other people had already carried statues out of the church, and when he imitated them, he found he had offended the Council, and now he is exiled. Help him, unless what we heard at the assembly where you were in charge, in criticism of the images, was not the Word of God. You can be of aid to him because of your education and great influence in St. Gallen."

But Conrad is more concerned, even disturbed, over what is happening at home in Zurich regarding the mass. As he has feared, although a month and a half have gone by since the disputation, no action has been taken. A spirit of unrest pervades Zurich. There have been demonstrations against the mass at the Great Church. The priests' assistants no longer want to perform the mass because the people mock them, and some of the prayer books are vandalized. The Council again calls together the commission that had sponsored the disputation, and asks them for recommendations. Zwingli and the other two city preachers ask for the right to conduct a service on Christmas without the mass, or, failing that, permission to distribute both the bread and the wine to the congregation. If even that is too much, they hope the Council will at least allow priests who have scruples of conscience against the mass to refrain from saying it.

Conrad, whose father brings home news from the commission's meetings, is bitterly disappointed. As it becomes obvious that Zwingli is consenting to move only as fast as the Council will allow. Conrad's heady sense of being led by the Word of God which stands above all human authority is fast dissipating. Where is the Zwingli who used to say that if the Council did not follow the Word it would be brushed aside by the irresistible tide of truth? Of all the people Conrad has looked to for a clear, defiant heralding of the truth, Zwingli has led the ranks. But now he seems to be softening under pressure.

When the Council's mandate has been drawn up, even before it can be issued, Conrad is already writing a biting letter to Vadian. "The cause of the gospel is in a very bad way here." Conrad minces no words. "It all started to go this way at the assembly where you were a presiding officer, when the Word of God was thrown down and trampled on by the ones who should have been its proclaimers, learned as they are. Now they have a commission of eight, including Zwingli and I don't know what other priestly monsters. Instead of obeying the divine teaching against saying mass they have shrewdly come up with a compromise, but it's a devilish one. It means that the mass is going to have to be said. Here is a saying you can quote: 'Whoever thinks or believes or says that Zwingli acts like a true Christian pastor thinks and believes and speaks wickedly.' I'll stand by that."

Bible-Studying Brothers

The gossip in the streets of Zurich in January 1524 is that only fourteen of the fifty members of the Small Council really favor the Reformation. But at the center of this body are a few moderates like Conrad Grebel's neighbor, Mayor Marcus Roist, who do lean toward Zwingli. To make sure that the smaller Council's foot-dragging will not slow the pace, the generally more Reform-minded Two Hundred pass a motion on January 11 stating that they will be the only judges of whether or not preachers are faithful to the gospel in their sermons. They keep the issue of the images alive by calling for still another discussion, and start to transfer some of the income from the tithes which has been going to the monasteries into a program of distributing soup and bread daily to the poor from the Dominican Cloister. Where the church has been lax in its charitable work, the Council now takes over.

Jacob Grebel is one of a committee of six which is asked to draw up plans for a total secularizing of the four Zurich monasteries, as well as the foundation of our Lady's Church, which supports seven Benedictine nuns. It is also to present suggestions for a new state system of social welfare.

The news from beyond Zurich is mixed. Vadian's town of St. Gallen has a Bible class, as of the first of the year, taught by a lay scholar in a private home. Their Council has copied Zurich by passing a decree that all preaching must limit itself to the Bible. Vadian is on a committee to judge any controversy on this matter. From Rome comes the report that the Pope considers Zurich to be infected with "the abominable Lutheran heresy." From Baden Conrad hears the shocking story that the shoemaker-iconoclast Claus Hottinger has been executed for speaking against the mass. And in nearby Witikon the radical preacher Wilhelm Reublin has gone on from protesting against the tithes to persuading some of his parishioners not to have their newborn babies baptized, claiming that a child cannot possibly repent before he comes to the age of reason. Soon the same thing happens in the hillside village of Zollikon, an hour's walk from Zurich, where John Brötli is pastor.

Now Zwingli is beginning to feel sufficient support for bolder moves. On April 2 he marries publicly the pregnant Anna Reinhard, whom he and his friends have considered his wife for two years. Under his leadership, one after another age-old "Christian" custom is dropped in Zurich. On Good Friday the image of Christ is not carried to the grave as formerly. The great annual procession of the men of Zurich to the shrine of the Virgin at Einsiedeln is abolished. The guilds no longer parade up to the Lindenhof carrying sacred relics.

But opinion is still divided in the Council and among the citizens. Zwingli is concerned that the town not split openly into parties. Already there are priests who will say mass and those who will not, people who venerate images and those who mock them. The possibility that Zurich could be partly Reformed and partly Catholic, as happened in Bohemia under the Reformer John Hus is unthinkable to Zwingli. The other cantons would then have a base within Zurich itself from which to crush the Reform. Zwingli is certain that it cannot be God's will for the gospel to be defeated. He is confident that if he dedicates himself completely to the establishment of the gospel in Zurich, his cause is God's, and God will make it as invincible as the Israel's armies of old, when they were obedient. From now the Old Testament preoccupies Zwingli. Most of his sermons, for the rest of his life, are based on its pages. There he finds the model of a people whose government is identical with their church, a pattern he believes to be the divine plan for all times.

Watching the political currents closely, Zwingli senses an opportune time for action when one of the mayors, the moderate Felix Schmidt, dies after a long illness, and the other one, Marcus Roist, also a moderate but favoring retention of images, is likewise at the point of death. Two days after Schmidt's death, and hours before Roist's, the Large Council announces that all images in Zurich's churches are now to be cleared out under government direction. Zwingli and other important persons will supervise to prevent any unnecessary damage.

In a few days the work begins. Locking the doors from the inside, with two constables standing by to keep order, the three leading priests, the master builder of the city, a master craftsman from each guild, and a crew of stonemasons, carpenters, and handymen strip the sanctuaries of their priceless religious art, now considered pagan. Propping ladders against the walls, workmen scratch off the paintings and apply whitewash. Zwingli rejoices: "Our temples in Zurich are indeed light." Stained glass, since it is not an object of worship, is allowed to remain.

Other changes follow. The organs are no longer played, traditional Catholic prayers are dropped; gold and silver cups and crosses are melted down; incense, banners, and crosses disappear; sacred garments are discarded (Zwingli has always worn his simple dark scholar's gown in the pulpit); and in the Great Church the bones of the city saints Felix and Regula are given a quiet burial.

The Catholic cantons of Switzerland are deeply angered and feel threatened by these moves. Many of their citizens clamor to have Zurich expelled from the Federation. This would expose the city to the mercy of Catholic Austria. In a town just south of the Rhine three pastors known to favor Zwingli are kidnapped by Catholic officials. A Reform-favoring crowd forms to rescue them. When its aim is frustrated, the unruly group storms into a nearby monastery, looting and wrecking it. Now Zwingli's opponents have another arguing point: he promotes lawlessness. Zwingli finds such a charge highly embarrassing to his campaign. Once again the trusted Jacob Grebel is placed on a committee to investigate the matter.

Where is Conrad Grebel in all of this change, and what are his thoughts? We find him and Barbara, now expecting their third child, still in the Grebel household. Recently they have been joined by one of Conrad's schoolmates, John Jacob Amman, who has married the fifteen-year-old "naughty little girl," Dorothea. It is not a good match; the marriage will be annulled in a year. When Dorothea becomes desperately sick a month after the wedding Jacob insists that Conrad write a hurried request for Vadian, the doctor, to come treat her. Conrad writes to Vadian on the day Zwingli's first child, a daughter, is born and named "Regula."

As for Zwingli's Reform program, Conrad is thinking troublesome thoughts. He feels deeply disappointed by something in the preacher's attitudes which he has not foreseen. He always imagined, as he sat with the eager scholars in Zwingli's house, that they were discovering together a divine Word that would sweep everything before it in the life of Zurich. Human wisdom and reservations would give way as the teaching and example of Christ were made the criterion of life. All other authority would have to take its place as the Word broke in.

It has been wonderful to see the first stages of this process. Zwingli's sermons have masterfully exposed the paganism not far beneath the surface of ordinary European Christianity. As opposition has developed, Zwingli has remained firm and infected his followers with his boldness. Sometimes he has cautioned his younger student, but there is no doubt about his total dedication to reclaiming the Christian gospel for all of Switzerland. His followers have begun to dream his dream. As the Council has gradually swung into line and begun to attack the old abuses, Conrad has been waiting with growing excitement for the final breakthrough, when Zurich will ringingly endorse the gospel en masse, and Christ will be Lord of all.

And then, last September, at a moment of decision, with the divine Word calling for a change, Zwingli gauged the mood of the Council, found it cautious, and decided he must let the Councillors set the timing of the Reform. Having called the mass an abomination according to the Scriptures, he turned out to be willing, in the face of threat to his program, to let it continue until the city government judges it is permissible to make the change.

Conrad is suddenly asking himself what right the magistrates have to tell the church of Christ when it may conform to the Scriptures. Zwingli says, "Be patient. The Word will take its course." But the more Conrad reflects on the situation, the more obvious it becomes to him that the Council has never had any real intentions of surrendering to any other authority the power it has gradually, for centuries, been taking over from the church. Zwingli, Conrad begins to believe, is naive to think they will ever let the Word rule completely. Or perhaps he no longer believes they will, and is playing along with their pragmatic ideas, rather than accepting the judgment of the eternal Word at any cost.

When Conrad and his friends first reason, then argue with Zwingli about his backing down under pressure, they taste the scorn he has previously heaped on the enemies of the gospel. Zwingli talks rapidly and, as Felix Mantz puts it, the opposing students feel their speech strangled in their throats. Conrad feels less and less respect for the man he has once so thoroughly admired. "Think of what will happen," Zwingli is saying, "if we push a perfectionist Christianity on a people who are only beginning to understand what Christ really taught! People must be made *ripe* for the gospel, as you have been." But what is the criterion, Conrad wonders: workability or the Word, political success or witness to the truth? Did Christ wait for the rulers of Jerusalem to schedule His witness? Was His kingdom subject to the administration of any human authority? Wasn't that what the cross was about — God's truth versus political "realities"? Who writes the agenda for the church? *Where* is the church?

Conrad and over a dozen other men in Zurich are now engaged in intense Bible study for themselves. Felix Mantz, in whose mother's house they hold their evening meetings, knows Hebrew. Conrad is tutoring pupils in Greek, and a crippled bookseller named Andreas Castelberger has a Bible class running regularly. Students, bakers, a pastor, a tailor, a goldsmith — they are fascinated, as they take the Scriptures into their own hands, to find Christ's teachings going beyond what they have learned from Zwingli. Reading both Old and New Testaments they discover that the New transcends the Old in its moral requirements, as well as its revelation of God through Christ. As Conrad searches eagerly, he fills to bursting with ideas. He challenges Zwingli: "When will you release the Christian church from its captivity to the public tax system? How can you be an employee of the city of Zurich and a free prophet of Christ? Who will break the news to the people that Christ calls on His followers to lay aside violence, even the common sword of self-defense? How long will you wait for the Council to let you abolish the repetitive sacrifice of the mass? What keeps you from giving up the baptizing of infants who can't possibly repent and believe the gospel? When will the rule of Christ become the rule of the church, whether or not the world is ready for it?"

Conrad waits for a public reply to his questions until he can hardly contain himself. He reads the latest pamphlets on issues of Reform and is excited to find two German authors — both former friends of Luther — who call for a much stronger discipline in the church than Zwingli, whom Conrad now regards as a compromiser. The one author, Andreas Karlstadt, has written on images and "false leniency," and argued that "every congregation should make up its own mind," instead of having decisions handed down to it by hierarchical officials. Thomas Müntzer, the other former Lutheran, has attacked false faith and called for a new church of the Spirit. He has also dared to criticize rulers who take advantage of the peasants.

Intrigued, Conrad and his friends decide to establish contact with both of these teachers as well as Luther himself. Perhaps they will be more approachable than Zwingli. The Zurich Bible students have not yet heard that Luther and Karlstadt openly quarreled in August, and that in the Black Bear Inn at Jena, the famous Reformer tossed a gold coin over a table at his former colleague Karlstadt, symbolizing a challenge to debate each other in print. But as he reads Karlstadt's writings, Conrad is heartened to find that his circle of Brothers are not alone in their forthright call for a new church with bold New Testament standards required of all members.

Vadian detects that Conrad is up to something, and writes to Jacob inquiring if Conrad may come to St. Gallen for a visit. After reading the letter, Jacob hands it to his son and asks him what he would like to do. "I'll go," Conrad says, but as he considers his health, the plans of his Bible-study group, and Barbara, who is pregnant, he decides instead to write Vadian a letter. "I'm writing to Andreas Karlstadt and Thomas Müntzer in reply to their books, and I expect also to write to Luther," Conrad tells Vadian. "I'm reading Matthew in Greek with some pupils, and finally (don't smile) I'm writing out my thoughts on two subjects and hope to publish them, unless someone else writes on my topics first." Conrad realizes that Vadian will be surprised to hear that he has suddenly decided to produce a book. "You wonder why I'm so bold," he writes. Then, revealing how much the Bible has become a part of his personality, he answers Vadian by quoting a speech from the Book of Job:

> I have waited, and they do not reply; they stand still and give no answer. I am going to contribute my part and tell what I know. Because I am so full of speech that the breath strains my belly, which is swelled as tight as a barrel of new wine without a vent. I must speak so I can breathe; I have to open my lips and answer them. I will not be im-

pressed with anyone's status, and I will not flatter anyone. If I did, God would take me away.

"Listen, you pastors!" Conrad scribbles feverishly.

He explains to Vadian why he has chosen not to make the trip. "I would rather communicate, if possible, by letter than have to leave my wife, my studies, and my projects. If the only purpose of my visiting you would be to eat together and have you entertain me, don't invite me anymore. Of course, if you consider it worthwhile, you can order me to come." An apologetic reminder of a tiny debt Vadian owes him shows, as the letter closes, how desperate Conrad's finances have become.

And now on behalf of the Bible study group Conrad completes his epistle to Thomas Müntzer. It is the longest letter he has ever composed, running to ten closely written pages. He addresses Müntzer in German instead of the scholarly Latin he uses for Vadian. Conrad knows little about Müntzer except what he has read in one book, so he begins by asking "Dear brother Thomas" not to be amazed at being addressed without any special title by people he has never heard of. "Jesus Christ," writes Conrad, "who calls us brothers, has motivated us to establish fellowship with you and call your attention to several topics.

"Just as our ancestors in the churches of Europe had given up Christ's true Word for human ceremonialism, which they trusted for salvation, until preachers like Zwingli came along, so now we still find 'Christians' who want a faith easy enough for everybody, including people who want to pay no price for their faith, who show no change of heart, who keep right on baptizing infants and repeating the mass. We were in the same mentality as long as we limited ourselves to listening to the new preaching, but when we took up the Scripture for ourselves we realized that both the preachers and we needed to pray urgently for deliverance from our human errors. What keeps the divine Word from going out clearly is the false leniency of these preachers. While we were bemoaning this, along came your book, and we were overjoyed to learn of someone else who understands these things. We want to urge and encourage you to hold to nothing but God's Word, rejecting every other opinion, even your own."

The first specific topic that Conrad takes up is the matter of singing in worship services. "We hear," he tells Müntzer, "that you have translated the mass into German, and that in celebrating it you use German chants. This cannot be good. . . ." Conrad wants no parts of the mass. He has been taught by Zwingli that the chanting of the service — hypnotizing the hearer by syllables of a language he does not understand — is a form of idolatry. Therefore, much as he loves music, Zwingli has wished to rule it out in the church entirely. Intensely eager to be thoroughgoing in reviving true worship, Conrad searches the New Testament for support, forcing on Paul's writings an interpretation that would forbid singing in public worship. In his ardor to hold to the Word, Conrad makes it say what it does not.

But when he moves from the marginal topic of singing at the mass to explaining his central understanding of the Lord's Supper, Conrad's thought is amazingly mature. He has been studying and thinking and discussing the matter for some time with his circle of Brothers. The meal which Christ left with the church, they now believe, is "a Supper of unity, not consecration." Ordinary bread and an ordinary cup should be used to turn the response from adoration of the bread to a sense of "becoming a part of the body of Christ and the brotherhood." Those who partake of the Supper must do so "in the Spirit and in love," and where faith and love do prevail, it will be a joyful experience, not a mysterious ritual. But if a person participates without a brotherly attitude, he condemns himself, because he does not understand what the meal is about. He fails to see how the cross of Christ teaches him to give himself to Christ and his brothers and sisters in Christ.

Further, Conrad writes to Müntzer, the Supper should not be "administered" to individuals. That is how Conrad feels the idea of mass developed in the first place — from individuals receiving communion. Actually, the Supper is in essence an expression of unity and not a "sacrament." Therefore, a person should not receive it alone, as on a deathbed. Nor should it be eaten in special sanctuaries, Conrad goes on. It should be eaten often, and never without obeying the Rule of Christ from Matthew 18.

Conrad is referring here to Christ's teaching that if there is a break in the fellowship of the brotherhood, the church must not fail to do something decisive about it in love. Such a situation involves more than someone's inner feelings, Conrad points out. If a member refuses to be reconciled with another member, he is to be left outside the fellowship — not taken along in the life of the church and the Lord's Supper as though nothing has happened. The Rule is actually based on love. It takes the church and the offender seriously. Without this Rule of Christ, Conrad writes, "it would not be the Lord's Supper. People keep the outward form, and the inner meaning — love — is let go." Conrad and his circle now feel that "it is much better that a few be taught right than that many people 'believe,' if that belief is false anyway."

A few lines of the letter discuss the problem of ministers who hesitate to preach doctrine that may get their salaries revoked, and thus present to their listeners an easygoing "sweet" Christ. The Zurich Brothers have also heard of a plan by Müntzer to replace images in his church with "tablets" containing the Ten Commandments, and they feel that this simply keeps alive the dependence on something external. It is better, they say, not to set up something new, but to organize a Christian church based solely on the principle taught in Matthew 18.

When discipline is needed in the church, only this Rule of Christ, not the "sword" of human force is to be used. "Right-thinking Christians are," as Zwingli himself formerly emphasized, "sheep among wolves."

Conrad agrees: "They must pass through anxiety, persecution and death to their heavenly rest, not by slaughtering their physical enemies, but by struggling with the spiritual enemies within themselves. They do not use the worldly sword, nor do they take part in war, because they have completely given up killing."

Conrad knows that the great Christian teacher Erasmus was a pacifist, and his followers, Zwingli and Conrad's friend Myconius, have also written against war. But the radical laymen of Zurich have now carried the teaching further. They know what they are requiring of their fellow Christians, since they expect that before long Zwingli may well use the sword of the "Two Hundred" to silence them. He can do this, because he says it is God's will that they not jeopardize the Reformation by asking the people to do more than they are yet ready to do for Christ.

Finally, Conrad writes that he and his Brothers appreciate

Müntzer's teaching on baptism, and wish to contribute several points to the discussion. Baptism, like the Lord's Supper, must be related to the Rule of Christ. That is, the person who is baptized must be held accountable by the church to prove by his new lifestyle that his sins have in truth been washed away. Otherwise, there is ceremony without content. The water itself is of no value, not a "comfort," as the professors of Wittenberg have said. And since it is not water that saves a person, there is no point in baptizing infants. Until individuals are old enough to choose between good and evil, they are saved without faith. "On the basis of many Scriptures we conclude that infant baptism is a senseless abomination."

Conrad realizes that this is a fundamental issue and hopes Müntzer is not tolerating infant baptism any longer. "If you or Karlstadt don't write further on this subject, I, Conrad Grebel, am going to try my hand at it. In fact, I have already begun. We are sure to be persecuted for this, more by the educated people than anyone else. Hold onto the Word alone." So far, Conrad has referred to the Word at least seventeen times in this letter. The Scriptures have become his life.

At the close of his epistle, Conrad expresses the eagerness of the Zurich Brothers for a reply from both Müntzer and Karlstadt. Adding a postscript, he says that he was going to write to Luther for the group, urging the famous Reformer not to pull back from strict discipline. However, Conrad notes, his affliction — perhaps the joints of his hands are inflamed again? — and the press of time have not permitted.

But while heavy September rains keep the letter carrier within the walls of Zurich for a while, Conrad finds time to write to Luther. The epistle to Müntzer is still lying on the table when a traveling goldsmith who is part of the Zurich fellowship, and who has recently visited Müntzer, arrives back in town. He has brought a book by Luther in which, as the Brothers see it, the famous Reformer has unfortunately "tied" his gospel to the control of the civil rulers.

The goldsmith has even more disturbing news. He reports that Müntzer has been preaching that where rulers do not yield to the progress of the gospel, Christians may overthrow them with violence.

"Is this true?" demands Conrad in a long postscript to the first letter. "If you and Karlstadt and the others to whom we have been

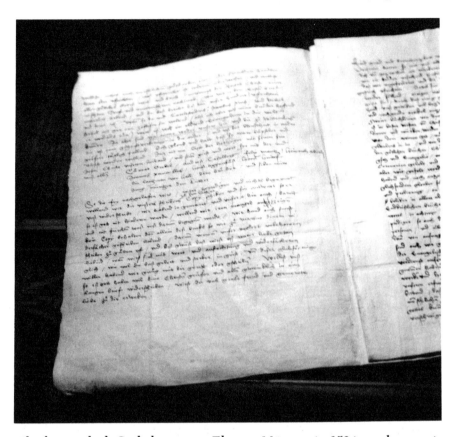

The letter which Grebel wrote to Thomas Müntzer in 1524 can be seen in the Vadian library in St. Gallen, along with correspondence between Conrad and Vadian, his prominent brother-in-law.

looking do not hold only to the Word and the Rule of Christ, it will be a miserable gospel that comes into the world. It's true that the educated preachers have opened up the gospel so that everyone hears about it, but people just take their word for what it is, and few read it for themselves. There aren't twenty of us here who believe the Word of God. Our preachers are so angry at us that they call us 'knaves' and 'disguised Satans' from the pulpit. We think it is only a matter of time before we are persecuted." In spite of this, Conrad adds, "We have admonished them."

Two new names are listed among the signers to this addition, and the letter is carried off. But there will be no reply, for by the time the messenger arrives at Thomas Müntzer's town, he has left, never to return. In a few months his name will be notorious on the lips of the worried rulers of Europe, and he will be dead along with hundreds of peasant followers, at the hands of the princes he has sought to overthrow in the name of Christ. Taking up the sword, he perishes with it. As for Luther, he can think of no adequate reply to Conrad's searching letter. But he does send word, through a friend, of his sympathetic interest in the Bible-studying Brothers in Zurich.

Karlstadt, to whom the bookseller Castelberger has written, does reply, sending along four new booklets from his pen, particularly on the Lord's Supper. The Brothers then send one of their members, Felix Mantz, to the printers at Basel, where he has Karlstadt's booklets published. A fifth book, on baptism, is considered by the Basel authorities too hot to allow through the press. Zwingli watches in dismay as the Brothers fill town and country with thousands of copies of Karlstadt's booklets. The emergence of a smaller movement, side by side with his more official campaign, strikes Zwingli as an almost greater danger than the conservative Catholic resistance. He feels that their effect is to discredit his hard-won point that he favors law and order, even though he has thrown off the traditional religious authority. To have come so far in the Reformation only to be threatened from the left by your most ardent former supporters infuriates him! Zwingli cannot recognize sincerity in such people.

Nor can Conrad Grebel, in him.

A Momentous Meeting

As winter's chill descends upon the Limmat, an atmosphere of change pervades the many-windowed Council Hall of Zurich. The magistrates, stepping carefully between critics, have decided that the time is ripe to close the detested monasteries permanently. The nuns across the river, both at Oetenbach and Our Lady's Church, make arrangements accordingly. The Dominican convent is sold to a nobleman. Catherine von Zimmern, ruler of her abbey since she was nineteen, gives the abbey and its vast forests to the city. A week later the monks, whose two monasteries stand a short walk in either direction from Conrad Grebel's front door, are likewise served notice. On December 10, with a heavy guard standing by, they are marched into the Franciscan Cloister. The young ones are notified that they must learn a craft like other citizens, unless they show a special aptitude for learning. Those too old to start over may retire in the monastery at the city's expense, but may no longer wear the monks' robes.

These touchy changes take place without much public protest, a subject that is now constantly on Zwingli's mind. The other cantons are pointing the finger at Zurich and its preacher, accusing them of troublemaking. Zwingli takes up his pen in defense in a booklet he entitles "Those Who Cause Disturbance." He sees no less than seven types of troublemakers, the first of which includes Conrad Grebel — radical evangelicals who are unwilling to tolerate Catholic abuses. Zwingli argues that this group disagrees with him only on nonessentials like timing. Among other troublemakers are the farmers who refuse to pay tithes, the priests, monks and nuns, the bishops, and those who oppose the baptizing of babies.

This book is Zwingli's public defense against his enemies in Switzerland, but he also has a private campaign under way. A Secret

Council has been formed, which is setting up a plan of war in case Zurich is attacked by the angry Catholic cantons. Zwingli, the evangelical preacher, helps to approve instructions concerning weapons and strategy, even down to appointing chaplains and designating trumpet signals. Conrad, whose father is never far from the Council's deliberations, hears rumors. "Zwingli is writing about 'disturbers,' " he tells Vadian. "It will probably hit us. Just see if something doesn't come of it." For months Conrad has been watching the process whereby Zwingli and the Council have arranged to support the progress of the gospel with the power of the civil sword. "They make a plan and not from God," he writes. "Hope is put in the help and strength of Pharaoh, but it will become a confusion and a disgrace."

When the busy Vadian lets over a month go by without a reply to such sentiments, Conrad guesses that he has offended his brother-in-law. Greeting him somewhat coldly as "Eminent Sir," Conrad writes a business note, reports the latest news, and then describes his current condition — severe debt. He comments further, "Almost no one in the whole Grebel clan is sympathetic to me. But I am getting used to it, and am taking it more calmly all the time. A Christian ought to be more concerned about his inner sins than external troubles."

It is almost customary for Conrad, in his current letters to Vadian, to call on Christ for patience, as though Conrad realizes that this is his weak point. "You don't believe," he fumes, "how it irritates me to watch the educated pastors, the leaders themselves, fouling the water which they lead their flocks to drink. That includes the main preacher, who is now calling me jealous and hypocritical and satanic. It's the same with him as with Luther: compromise, followed by expanding away the seriousness of it." The letter closes with the discouraged signature, "Conrad, a nobody, no longer a Grebelian."

While Conrad's reputation is sinking in Zurich, Vadian's is rising in St. Gallen. As city doctor, he finds his voice increasingly respected. In little more than a year he will be the town's chief official. Just now he is concerned with some outdoor Bible lectures being given by a local guildmaster's son, Ulimann, who has recently returned as a monk from a monastery in another canton. The

Council has asked the previous teacher, an educated layman, to stop holding the classes, because division was setting in. The iconoclast Hochrutiner, whom Conrad Grebel recommended a year ago, has been criticizing infant baptism in the classes. But as soon as the meetings stopped Ulimann has started them up again under a linden tree beside St. Mangen's Church.

As the winter cold becomes more bitter, the crowds clamor to be let into the church for their classes. They try to force the door but it holds. Council knows there must be decisive action as they hear reports of strident preaching and quotations from letters of Conrad Grebel. They issue a mandate allowing only priests to teach in the churches, but soften the blow by renewing permission for private classes. Ulimann, a firebrand, soon has crowds gathering in the large hall of the weavers' guild in which his father holds the rank of master.

As Vadian, who regards himself as Reform-minded, is trying to find a path of moderation through these stormy events, another letter is brought to him from his puzzling young brother-in-law. It opens with the hottest issue in both their cities — infant baptism. "Some people here who understand God's truth on this question," Conrad writes, "do not want to have their children baptized. Milords have warned them, but they are standing firm, and have asked for justice, appealing to the Bible. Then both Small and Great Councils have commanded the opponents of infant baptism to present their ideas before the three city pastors and four Council members. Zwingli took the least sophisticated of these men and dealt with him singly, but he stood up against their intelligence successfully. Now more general discussions have been ordered."

For almost a year now Council has had trouble with this issue. In August they sent Pastor Wilhelm Reublin to jail, and fined the nonbaptizing parents of his parish, but the question has refused to die down. Vadian has not yet made up his mind on it. Conrad, whose wife, Barbara, expects a baby within the month, has for some time considered infant baptism an abomination.

Halfway through the letter Vadian receives an unpleasant jolt. Conrad is sternly questioning his prosperous brother-in-law's obedience to the gospel: "Achieving financial advantage brings us, at best, a temporary happiness in this world, and it can often disguise the naked force which supports it. It is impossible to reconcile the love of money with God's truth." Conrad is implying that Vadian hesitates to obey God because he does not want to endanger his economic position! The cheek of this fellow! He goes on: "I believe the Word of God without a complicated interpretation, and out of this belief I speak. May God give you the mercy to submit to His Word without reservations, and obey it. Otherwise, things probably don't stand as well with us as we might hope. The way is narrow."

Vadian is at a loss to understand this kind of expression from his formerly admiring friend. The doctor prefers a more reasonable and respectful approach. Conrad betrays a dangerous urgency: "God is the Judge of our so-called 'faction' here in Zurich. They call us disturbers. We'll find out by their actions who the real disturbers are when they begin to expel and execute people. I don't expect them to refrain from persecution. I hope to God that He will give us the patience to take it."

Before he closes this bristling letter, Conrad sends greetings to the Bible study pupils in St. Gallen, with whom he knows Vadian partly sympathizes. He also mentions "the beginners in the Word of God and the godly life," asking them to pray for their evangelical friends in Zurich. "I have spoken the truth here according to the Scriptures," Conrad concludes. "Take it in the same spirit. Conrad Grebel, your sincere brother-in-law. I would prefer that we were brothers agreed in the truth of Christ."

Vadian shakes his head and decides that Conrad is being carried away by his temper. The "discussions" Conrad and his friends have had with Zwingli recently on infant baptism must have polarized him, along with Felix Mantz, who is claiming that Zwingli does not argue fairly. Felix insists on presenting his testimony on the question to the Council in written form, because otherwise Zwingli overpowers him with fast talking. And perhaps Vadian does not yet know that a priest from Ulimann's monastery, also a son of thunder, is now in Zurich, where he finds Zwingli too compromising, and is now attending the meetings of Conrad's circle. This priest's name is Georg Cajacob.

A few days after Christmas, the busy doctor of St. Gallen pens a short letter to Conrad. "I'm surprised," he begins, that you jump to the conclusion that I enjoy criticizing you. I don't. I only wish, as

Dr. Joachim von Watt, his name Latinized to Vadian, was Grebel's teacher, friend, and brother-in-law. Vadian became mayor of St. Gallen and an important figure in the history and development of that Swiss city.

I have all along, that you would behave with more respect to Zwingli and Leo Jud and not be so foolishly argumentative. They're making it their business to advance the Word, and they aren't free to get rid of abuses overnight that have built up over many years." Give the whole matter some time, Vadian argues. Baptism, like the other disputed questions, will be brought into line with the Word eventually. Peace and concord are what Vadian wants. But if Conrad insists on a complete and immediate resolution, "I can't prevent you or the others." Still, Vadian closes good-naturedly, "I'd like to give you my advice, as a relative, to show more discretion and meekness." Vadian displays this spirit himself by adding, "I'm ready to be taught, if I have a wrong understanding of these matters."

By now Conrad is seriously exasperated. From all sides, whenever he and his friends ask to have the practice of infant baptism compared with scriptural teaching, they are lectured about being reasonable. Zwingli's new booklet on disturbers offers the astonishing explanation that the basis for baptizing infants in the New Testament is the commandment to circumcise in the Old. This is reasonable? As Hans Hottinger, one of the town watchmen, is heard to remark, "I don't know what to make of Zwingli's preaching; today he says one thing and tomorrow he takes it back. He preached a few years ago that infants shouldn't be baptized; now he says they should." That may be tolerable as street talk, but Hottinger is in trouble when he is quoted further: "If Zwingli says that God has commanded us to baptize children he lies like a rogue and a heretic."

This is not moderate language, but the Grebel circle has now begun to fear something more weighty than Zwingli's displeasure. Conrad is coming to the dread conclusion that the kingdom of God, demanding man's total obedience, is not nearly as welcome in Zurich as he has imagined. It is calling him counter to the very Reformers he has heretofore trusted with his soul. As he prays and reads the New Testament with his friends an overwhelming sense of God's judgment on their half-loyalties begins to grow. He would never have guessed that the whole confrontation would center on infant baptism as a prime issue, but there it is. One can stay away from mass without penalty, and the images are gone. Yet after all this, Zurich's reformed Council is going to demand, with the power of the sword, that its citizens perform a ceremony some of them believe to be anti-Christian. Conrad finds it preposterous. That Christian shepherd — Zwingli!

On Friday, January 5, 1525, Conrad and Barbara welcome into their family a tiny new daughter, giving her the biblical name of Rachel. Five days later in an open discussion before the council, Conrad, Felix Mantz, Georg Cajacob, and Wilhelm Reublin are challenged on the question of resisting infant baptism. A twenty-year-old minister, newly arrived in Zurich, joins Zwingli in facing them. His name is Heinrich Bullinger. He will one day take Zwingli's place as head of the church in Zurich, and will write the disparaging account that will cheapen Conrad's reputation for centuries. As the debate warms he is astounded to observe the boldness of the accused. To his diary he confides, "Their impertinence is amazing!"

Now the pace quickens. Within 48 hours of the discussion one of the radical Hottingers interrupts a sermon on the topic of infant baptism in the Zurich Hospital. The episode is fairly mild, and the Council is not sure how to respond. But the populace is tense. On the day following, a Friday, Conrad hears Zwingli preach a political sermon so forceful that the congregation breaks into applause. On Saturday he writes to Vadian that he will again be facing Zwingli in debate on the coming Tuesday night. "Tomorrow," Conrad notes, "a proclamation will be made inviting all persons, lay or clergy, with an interest in the question of infant baptism, to speak before the assembled Councils." As for Rachel, she is eight days old but has still not been baptized in the idolatrous "Romish bath," as Conrad puts it. He reminds Vadian, also, to look into a small financial matter for him. With four mouths to feed he says he is "desperately in need."

The Council has no intention of providing Conrad, Felix, Georg, and Wilhelm with so large an audience for their ideas after the next Tuesday evening. Zwingli, in fact, considers it dangerous to have his authority questioned so vehemently in public. In particular, he finds Georg Cajacob, so new in town that in the discussions he is referred to simply as "the one in the blue coat," to be unacceptably "wild" in his manner. The nickname sticks; Georg is known henceforth as "Bluecoat" (*Blaurock*).

The result of the Tuesday night discussion is a foregone conclusion. On Wednesday the Council announces that all infants in the

103

canton of Zurich who have not been baptized must have the ceremony administered to them within a week. Otherwise, their parents
are to be expelled with their children and goods. Little Rachel
Grebel is nearly two weeks old and still unbaptized. On the following day Zwingli writes the news of the decision to Vadian, with
the observation that Conrad "still persists in his stand, together with
a few other less important people." Zwingli is anxious lest such a
spirit spread. "Tell the brothers at St. Gallen," he writes, "not to
make a great to-do by rejecting infant baptism."

As Saturday, January 21, 1525, dawns over Conrad Grebel's
city, its rulers have not yet finished with the stubborn Bible students. Assembling by the Limmat under the chairmanship of Diet-
helm Roist, the richest citizen in town, they take counsel together to
put teeth into their new law on baptism. Zurich must be protected
from radicals. The four men in the Grebel circle who do not hold
citizenship in the canton must get out within a week. Georg Bluecoat, still not fully understood, is not mentioned, but Conrad and
Felix are. They may hold no more of their gatherings, may not discuss the question of baptism openly, and no more disputations will
be granted them. If they have matters of faith to discuss, they can
see the mayor or one of his three assistants. The announcement
falls on the group like a sledgehammer.

Darkness is falling on this same Saturday night as sixteen saddened men gather quietly in the home of Felix Mantz, a few minu-
tes' walk from the Great Church Square. Their mood is solemn. This
is a forbidden meeting. Within a week four of them must be gone,
including one of their main teachers — Andreas Castelberger, nicknamed "On the Crutches." The severe consequences of their stand
are now clear. The Christian city of Zurich will no longer tolerate
their testimony and has publicly branded them a disgrace to the town.
As they ponder their next move, it is suggested that they should
have a baptismal service here and now, irrevocably separating themselves from the world which now stands ready to persecute them in
the name of Christ. Georg Bluecoat, in particular, is ready to make
the momentous move.

But fear presses on their hearts. Conrad knows all too well that
such an act may cost him the little earthly treasure he has left —
the precious Zurich citizenship in which he could raise his family in

*The Neustadtgasse in Zurich, directly behind the Grossmunster and just up-
hill from Zwingli's parsonage. The Anabaptist movement began in earnest on
January 21, 1525, when believers' baptism was shared among a number of
persons at a Bible study in the home of Felix Mantz located on this street.*

honor and peace. After a searching discussion the men kneel to pray. When they rise the man in the blue coat turns, not toward the two pastors present, but to his new friend, Conrad Grebel, the natural leader in their strange new fellowship. The 33-year-old priest makes a tense appeal: "Conrad, I beg you, for God's sake, give me the true Christian baptism!" It is a moment without precedent since Charlemagne settled the Christian faith on the tribes of Europe with the sword that rests across his imperial knees in the sculpture on the tower of the Church of Christ in Zurich. For seven centuries since, Christian baptism has been administered to the innocent babies of the Swiss tribes, passing on the cult, whether or not there was repentance. These men know this well. They realize what they are doing. They count the cost.

The priest confesses his faith in Christ. Conrad Grebel reaches for water. As he pours it on the bowed, balding head of this fiery disciple, he cannot know that in this act is inaugurated a fellowship that shall spread beyond Europe to every continent. And now Georg himself moves around the circle, baptizing each upon his request. They commission each other to carry the gospel of Jesus Christ to their world, and covenant in an unshakable bond to keep the faith. Conrad Grebel and his Brothers, whether Zwingli or Council or bishop approve or not, are now preachers of the gospel. Their church is subject to no authority but Christ. It is not Zwingli's, nor the priest's, but a believers' church.

Determined to Testify

As the early evenings fall on the frozen hillside streets of Zollikon, a glow of torches is visible sporadically. They are carried to hastily called meetings in farmhouses by a group of tailors, shoemakers, wine-growers, students, and non-assigned pastors. Zurich's Council has not given permission for such meetings, nor has it occurred to the participants to ask. At one of the gatherings, Conrad Grebel stands at a table surrounded by a roomful of local men. He reads not from a civil mandate, but from the New Testament — the account of Christ's Last Supper. He explains that they are about to eat a meal of brotherhood in memory of Christ's death for their sake. This will show that they have committed themselves to a new life. Then he shares both the loaf and the cup with his friends, in the simplest manner possible.

Conrad himself has less than a week to get out of his native Zurich, unless he intends to let his baby daughter Rachel be baptized. He has no intention of going back to this practice. Every day his situation becomes more tense. In the house of Felix Mantz he finds an excited visitor from Vadian's St Gallen. On hearing the news of the new fellowship in Zurich, he has felt called by the Holy Spirit to come and request true Christian baptism. Conrad fulfills the man's desire. Other baptisms are administered in Zollikon all week long, performed by a farmer and a tailor's apprentice, as well as the pastors Brötli and Reublin, both of whom have been ordered to leave the canton.

Daily the Lord's Supper is shared. A wooden dish and a simple dipper are used to pour the water on those being baptized. But after only a few days Conrad is missing from the fellowship. Leaving a lonely Barbara and his three little children — Theophilus, not yet three; Joshua, a year and a half; and Rachel, at her mother's breast

— Conrad is heading north to the city of Schaffhausen. Conrad believes he can find a sympathetic ear among the pastors in this town where the Rhine pours its massive cascades over Europe's most majestic waterfall. He knows that vigorous leaders like Georg Blaurock can carry on the work among Zollikon's farmers in his absence.

Within a week Zurich's authorities have had enough of this free Christianity. It all comes to a head when Blaurock (Bluecoat) blocks the local pastor from mounting the pulpit at Zollikon on Sunday morning. "What do you intend to do?" he demands.

Amazed, Pastor Niklaus Billeter, assigned to this church by the Great Church organization in Zurich, answers, "Preach the Word of God."

Blaurock disagrees. "You haven't been sent to preach. *I* have!"

The pastor brushes off the unexpected protest, walks into the pulpit, and begins his sermon, but Georg keeps interrupting. Now Billeter realizes he has a possible uproar on his hands, and turns toward the door. Persons in the congregation call out to him to return, and he does, requesting that any criticisms be brought to him privately.

But Georg isn't finished. Banging his stick on a bench, he quotes, "My house shall be called a house of prayer, but you have made it a den of thieves!" Now a local official stands up and informs Georg that if he does not quiet down he will be taken to jail.

In 24 hours police from the city of Zurich move through Zollikon, rounding up the farmers who have been baptized during the past week, along with Georg and Felix Mantz. The two ringleaders are imprisoned in the jail tower in the Limmat, while space is found in the recently emptied Augustinian monastery of Zurich for the 25 farmers. There Zwingli and the other two city pastors, along with Council members, question them. The converts feel pleased to hear Zwingli say that he too hopes to make changes to bring Zurich's church more into line with biblical teaching, though he does not approve of their unofficial actions. After a week they are fined and released, on condition that they not meet in groups of more than three or four. They may read the Bible and discuss it, but baptism, the Lord's Supper, and preaching must be left strictly to the official pastors. Georg and Felix, who are not so easily influenced, are kept in jail to make sure they do not stir up more trouble.

Throughout the first momentous week in the history of the Swiss Brothers numerous meetings for worship and witness were held in Zurich and Zollikon. One of these took place on Rudi Thomann's farm on the Gstadtrasse in Zollikon on January 25, 1525.

By this time Brötli and Reublin, the two expelled pastors, have reached Schaffhausen, where they find Conrad Grebel already at work. He is in contact with the two leading pastors, both influential doctors of theology, who realize that Conrad is no intellectual fly-by-night. Dr. Sebastian Hofmeister, the head pastor, was at both disputations called by Zurich the year before last, and Conrad observed that he was unusually sympathetic to the Reformation. Perhaps here, where Zwingli is not an immediate threat, there will be freedom to teach against infant baptism and to call out a believers' church like the one in Zurich and Zollikon. The conversations are excitingly promising. One evening both doctors sit down in Hofmeister's home not only with Conrad but with Brötli and Reublin as well. Hofmeister is so nearly convinced that he is ready to tell the Schaffhausen Town Council that there is no biblical support for infant baptism. Conrad shares with them a list of scriptural passages he has collected on the topic. Encouraged, Brötli and Reublin move on the next day to the town of Hallau, where before long Brötli baptizes nearly the whole adult community. Reublin goes up the Rhine to make contact with the well-known pastor Dr. Balthasar Hubmaier, who has now come out against baptizing infants, but has not been baptized as an adult himself.

Almost immediately, however, Zwingli is on their trail. A letter arrives in Schaffhausen from the Zurich Council telling of the recent debates with Conrad's group, and of their expulsion. Further, the letter reads, Zwingli has begun an important new book, *On Baptism, Infant Baptism, and Rebaptism,* to warn people against them. The news triggers a reaction. Schaffhausen's Council assures Zurich at once that they are not, as rumored, going to have a public debate on baptism, and the next day they issue a mandate commanding that all babies be baptized. The civil authorities intend to follow the Zurich pattern. Dr. Hofmeister now begins to back off from Conrad's ideas. Something similar occurs with a French nobleman now in town, whom Conrad recently met in Zurich, and who is now eagerly looking into the Bible for himself. He tells Conrad, who has surprised him with his sharp criticisms of Zwingli, that he is going to talk to Zwingli himself to see if these things are true. Still another promising contact occurs when Ulimann, the irrepressible Bible teacher arrives from St. Gallen looking for Conrad, asks to be taught, and then insists on being immersed naked in the wintry Rhine.

Conrad is saddened when he hears that the Zollikon brothers, in return for their release, have promised not to preach. But soon there is more encouraging news. Georg Blaurock has been set free (only Felix Mantz is still jailed), and he begins to baptize people on the very next day, stirring up the movement again. Leaving Pastor Billeter unmolested in his Zollikon church this time, Georg preaches and baptizes in the crowded rooms of a nearby farmhouse. Then, sensing danger, he disappears. But a local farmer, Jorg Schad, baptizes forty people in the Zollikon church itself. In every meeting they eat the Lord's Supper together. The church of Christ, beholden to no one but their Lord, is appearing!

Once again the constables of an alarmed Zurich sweep through the town. This time they imprison each offender in a separate cell and Zwingli talks to them individually. To excuse their apparent breaking of their oath of peace, they argue that it was given in Zurich, while they have done their baptizing in Zollikon. After nine days all but four are ready to promise again to stop these activities.

About the time of their release, Conrad slips back into town. His campaign in Schaffhausen has not succeeded. The French nobleman who went to see Zwingli has come back ill and angry. Before he died he blasted Conrad with the accusation that he had misled him about Zwingli. "I thought Zwingli would infect you with his poison," Conrad replied. And now in Zurich the news is equally depressing. Only four of those most recently arrested have stuck to their testimony under pressure. The others promise not to baptize anyone nor to speak against baptizing infants. Conrad decides to go to a more promising field, where he has connections, and where Wolfgang Ulimann, whom Conrad baptized, is again teaching enthusiastic crowds in the hall of the weavers' guild.

Conrad leaves his family and Zurich so quietly that Zwingli, who noted his arrival with alarm, does not at first realize he is gone. What the Reformer heard about Conrad's position from the French nobleman has deeply offended him. "Grebel is with us," he writes quickly to Vadian, who by this time has doubtless welcomed Conrad to St. Gallen, "and is drawing everyone he can to his party by slandering and libeling us so much that even if we were as bad as he says we are, it would be very improper for him to be so ungrateful to us after all he has gotten from me. Beware of being misguided by his propaganda. He has the habit of not mentioning what I say, while he fills your ears with his own stuff."

But by the time the letter arrives Conrad has been drawing packed houses at the weavers' guild, where he is preaching the gospel in an atmosphere of favorable excitement. St. Gallen is in ferment. Many of the common citizens have resented for years the economic burdens they help to carry for the great monastery around which the town has always existed. Vadian cautiously observes, knowing that his advice will be decisive in the response of the St. Gallen Council to the new movement. Everyone in town realizes that the popular young teacher is none other than the brother-in-law of their famous Vadian.

As Conrad calls daily for repentance and a new life, people begin to respond. Holy Week is near and Palm Sunday is approaching, which has been in years past the day for a colorful religious procession. Some towns have a centuries-old custom of trundling through their streets a wooden statue on wheels of Christ riding a donkey. But this year St. Gallen witnesses a new Palm Sunday event. People crowd the highway leading from town in the direction of Zurich. They are following Conard Grebel to the dramatic gorge of the Sitter River nearby, to be baptized into the kingdom of God. There in a kind of fulfillment he could hardly have hoped for, he takes one Swiss citizen after another into the waters of repentance. As he lays his crippled hands on their willing shoulders, he must be calling to mind the scene at the Jordan River 1,500 years ago. It is simply not true, as Zwingli argues, that the people are not ready to accept the gospel. Given the freedom to listen to it, as here in St. Gallen, they press into the kingdom without any Council or priest to tell them they may or may not. In fact, whatever unwillingness is evident is shown by the officials of the government and church, not the people. Some 500 have now been baptized in St. Gallen, and in a week 300 of Balthasar Hubmaier's parishioners, together with their pastor, will receive the same rite at the hands of Conrad's friend Wilhelm Reublin.

But during all this excitement Zwingli is moving forward steadily too. A new Board, including Jacob Grebel, has been formed to set up laws concerning marriage and moral behavior, now that the Bish-

Life-size figures of Mary, Joseph, Christ, and the saints were part of the seasonal pageantry and visual aids to medieval Christian education. Each year on Palm Sunday this Christ made his triumphal entry in the Canton of Schwyz.

op's control over Zurich's religious life has been eliminated. The Council will take over the supervision of punishment for religious offenses like blasphemy, immodest dress, or sexual misbehavior. Zwingli is also hard at work on plans for a biblical college to be set up in the Great Church, where new ministers can be taught Hebrew and Greek. But a more obvious change occurs two days after Conrad's baptisms in the Sitter. Zwingli, feeling that at last he has the backing of the majority of the officials, goes before the Zurich Council and demands that the mass no longer be said in their churches. He has prepared a new German liturgy for the Lord's Supper, and a new ceremony for baptizing infants. The Council is indeed ready, and on Wednesday, April 12, 1525, finally discards what Conrad Grebel has found intolerable for the last year and a half. On Thursday, for the first time since the Great Church was built seven centuries before, the language of the people is used with the bread and wine. After praying and preaching, Zwingli shares with an immense gathering a simple Lord's Supper. As Conrad and his band of Brothers have now been doing for months, Zwingli and his two deacons share the wine as well as the bread with all who participate.

Conrad has left St. Gallen, and in his place Bolt Eberli, an eloquent, good-hearted man, is preaching from the Scriptures and baptizing believers in fields and houses near the city. The St. Gallen Council has begun to worry, and Vadian calls Bolt to his house to break the news in a friendly way that his presence is no longer desired. Bolt obeys in a cooperative spirit, but immediately Conrad's friend Ulimann gathers crowds just outside the city gates. The Council summons him and asks him to leave too or be banished in three days. Not everybody who listens to the new preaching, it is clear, is of a peaceful spirit. Fanatics are beginning to appear. News that some peasants have plundered a nearby monastery arrives in the middle of the excitement.

Conrad, on his way back to Zurich and his family, realizes that not everyone who is dissatisfied with the authorities is ready for baptism. When a man in whose home he stops briefly asks what a person must do to be baptized, Conrad answers, "First you have to give up your woman-chasing, gambling, drinking, and money-grabbing." As for Vadian, he has begun to feel that the new movement led by his brother-in-law is dangerous. Conrad believes that Vadian agrees with his teaching, but he fears that the prosperous doctor will side with the opponents of the gospel to remain respectable.

Once he is back in Zurich, Conrad slips into his home and stays off the street to avoid being caught and banished. As long as that does not happen, he has not, technically, lost his citizenship in the canton. He is delighted to have a secret visitor — Felix Mantz, who has escaped from jail in the past two weeks with twenty other members of the new fellowship. Conrad and Felix talk over their exciting plans to expand the testimony which has now taken root in three or four towns. Felix plans to visit Georg Blaurock's home district. Conrad decides to leave the city with him, but he has not reckoned with Barbara. Having been without a husband almost all of the past three months, she is in no mood to watch him set out again on a secret mission. As she sees him preparing to leave after dark on a Sunday evening, she threatens to report Felix to the authorities. Conrad still feels that he must go. Tearing himself away from her urgent pleas, he starts out a door. In desperation she dashes out another and bursts into Jacob Grebel's quarters, crying that Conrad is leaving again.

By now Conrad is hobbling on aching feet toward the New Market Gate, trying to avoid recognition. As he might have known, the gate is shut for the night, so he creeps by the defunct Franciscan Monastery to the next gate, the Lindentor, and knocks at the watchman's house. And as he has feared, a woman recognizes him and calls from her window that no one is let out at night through that gate. He knows this well enough, and so, limping painfully, he goes to try the New Market Gate once more. As he walks along he prays for guidance, realizing that if he is caught and banished, or if Felix is betrayed by Barbara, guards will be posted and he will no longer be able to visit his friends in Zurich and Zollikon.

There is no escape from the city tonight, and Felix leaves without Conrad. Although everyone now knows he is at home, no one disturbs him, and some of the Brothers visit him, bringing the news that Zwingli's new book on baptism is on Froschauer's printing press. Conrad finds that the arguments he has used against infant baptism in Schaffhausen have been handed to Zwingli. He wishes he could write a public answer to Zwingli, though he knows that would risk his citizenship. As he stays at home, looking out a window where people in the marketplace can see him, but not daring to go out, he realizes that he must find some money somewhere. All he owns that is salable is his collection of textbooks. Perhaps, he thinks, when the new college begins, someone might at least be willing to buy the Greek books. He decides to write to his book-selling friend Andreas Castelberger, giving him a list of his books. If he can find a prompt purchaser, Conrad writes, he will throw in some of the books at no cost. He is now at the end of the line financially.

At the end of the letter Conrad turns to the matter foremost in his mind, Zwingli's cooperation with the government to suppress the Brothers. Using figures from the Book of Revelation, which he has just been reading, he writes: "These ministers are making war against the Lamb of God, but the Lamb will overcome in His own time. In the meantime, good-bye in the peace and patience of the Lord."

While pondering his next move, Conrad hears disturbing news from St. Gallen. The Council there, thoroughly alarmed, has demanded a written defense from both the Brothers and their opponents, the city pastors. Action will soon be taken. Vadian himself is writing a little "book" against the "Baptizers." At the same time the fantastic story arrives in Zurich that Thomas Müntzer, who never received the lengthy letter Conrad wrote, has led an army of peasants in open revolt against their lords. Philip of Hesse has crushed them, with 5,000 deaths. Such horrors only fix in conservative minds a fear of change, and Conrad's radical fellowship is seen by men in authority as part of the same general unrest. No matter that Conrad has warned Müntzer solemnly against bloodshed. For hundreds of years critics will glibly number Conrad among his followers.

Zwingli, well aware of the upcoming confrontation in St. Gallen, has dedicated his new book to that city, hoping to swing its people into opposition to the Brothers, or Anabaptists ("Rebaptizers") as they are now called. (Their friends call them Baptizers in agreement that their first infant baptism had not been a true one and that their adult baptism was, in that sense, not a rebaptism.) On the day after the new marriage law of Zurich is finally passed by the Council, Zwingli receives his book from Froschauer's, and immediately sends a shipment to St. Gallen. With it goes a letter to Vadian, asking him to do all he can to put down the Rebaptizers, "the enemies of the gospel." We are in a struggle to the death with them, Zwingli writes. "Warn your Council in our name that there can be no greater opposition to the gospel than this rebaptism." Dealing with these people is such a tricky business, Zwingli confides, that he has not told his wife much about their affairs. As he views it, the reason the Brothers insist on baptizing people is that this enables them to get people into their own faction.

Conrad, too, is keeping in close touch with the situation in St. Gallen. A showdown there, like the earlier one in Zurich between the Brothers and the town officials, is only a few days off. Deeply anxious over the outcome, Conrad feels that he must confront Vadian as never before. When he sits down in agitation to write the letter, he has not yet heard the worst — that just yesterday the preacher Bolt Eberli was burned at the stake by the Catholic authorities at Lachen. But he feels the tension and knows the stakes are high.

"Greetings to you and peace in the Lord, not in the world," he addresses Vadian, more as a brother in Christ than a brother-in-law. Conrad realizes that any criticism he offers will be met with the accusation of ingratitude. "I'm very thankful," he begins, "for all the kind things you have done for me. I couldn't wish for more." Now Vadian will know something serious is coming.

"But I have to be free to say to you what must be said. You still have not been willing to listen to the teachings of the Spirit more than to the voice of the flesh. I realize that you know this, but I will say it here. If any punishment, such as prison, fine, banishment, or death is decided on against my Brothers, it will be entirely or at least very largely your own responsibility."

The failed student now makes an impassioned appeal to his successful brother-in-law, whose moderate voice carries weight in the councils of St. Gallen: "Beware! Beware of innocent blood! Because it is innocent, whether or not you acknowledge it to be. Their patience and character and God's judgment will bear this out eventually. Unless you recover your wits, your learning and your dignified position will only hasten your own destruction. I call heaven and earth to witness! I beg you to bear with me as I say this, which is the truth of Christ. If God wills, I shall testify to the death to this truth, in which the Brothers are, and you could be too."

Even if he has been able to take all this with friendly feeling,

117

Vadian will be stung by Conrad's next thrust: "I know what is moti-
vating you: money, or fleshly 'wisdom,' or Zwingli's politics. Don't
destroy yourself, I beg you. You may deceive men, but not God. Get
out of the wealth-game; trust God and be humble enough to be satisfied with little. Pull out of Zwingli's bloody party. Run from your
own wisdom to God's; be a fool to the world but wise to Him. Become like a little child; otherwise you cannot enter the kingdom of
God."

Conrad's loyalty to this kingdom is now so complete, and his
faith in its triumph so sure that he feels a terrible pity for Vadian,
as well as for the Brothers whom Vadian may help to suppress. "If
you don't want to stand with the Brothers, at least don't resist
them, so that your guilt will be less, and don't give other communities an example of persecution."

In his days as a student, Conrad has often written playfully,
"by Jove." Now he has a different language of emotion. "By my
faith in Christ, by heaven and earth and whatever they contain, I
tell you sincerely that I have rebuked you here like this only out
of love. I adjure you through Christ, don't despise me as I warn you
from Him. Take it as a call to recover your wits. If you yield, I'll
lay down my life for you; if you won't, I'll lay it down for my
Brothers. I'll testify in giving up my possessions, and even my home,
which is all I have, in prison, exile, or death, and in public writing,
if God allows. And if I don't write, there will be others who will."

Still Conrad can't stop; he hopes against hope that Vadian
might yet be persuaded to come out publicly on the side of the
Brothers. "You agree with our teaching; Zwingli disagrees. What
are you waiting for, an excuse to reject it, and even to persecute
us? My dear Vadian, why don't you testify along with us? Why do
you use the power of the state, twisting the Scriptures against us?
Do you think we are crazy, or demon-possessed? We are ready to
testify to the death — which it is evident Zwingli and others are
preparing for us. . . ."

The real difference that is opening up between them, Conrad
suggests as he closes, is that Brothers will place their lives on the
line. "The teaching of the Lord has been given for the purpose of
being put into practice," not merely affirmed as true. Without a
commitment to do that at any cost, Vadian will not be able to under-

The heart of St. Gallen as it appears today. While a few of the homes and the church on the right predate Vadian's time, the monastery has since been rebuilt and embellished in baroque style.

stand what the Brothers are about. Yet Conrad is able to ask the doctor to pray for him, "and I in turn shall pray for you as a brother without ceasing. Be patient with me and be on your guard. Farewell in the Lord Jesus Christ." The letter is addressed "To Joachim Vadianus, my brother-in-law and brother in the Lord." When Vadian has read it and disapprovingly tucked it away with the more than fifty others he has received from Conrad since the days when they were professor and student in Vienna, he does not realize that the collection is now complete. There will be no more. And Vadian has made up his mind that Conrad has lost contact with reality. It is time to restore order in St. Gallen.

On the following Sunday, Pentecost of 1525, the pastor of St. Lawrence's Church in St. Gallen announces that Zwingli's book will be read from his pulpit that evening. A large audience, including many who have responded to Conrad's preaching, packs the house. As they listen to the schoolmaster read Zwingli's argument that baptism takes the place of circumcision, and is thus the sign of belonging to a family rather than of individual choice, Wolfgang Ulimann rises and shouts, "You can have Zwingli's word. We want the Word of God!"

The reader responds that this is God's Word as explained by Zwingli.

"Then let us hear Conrad Grebel's explanation too!" shout several in the crowd. "We have a letter from him that speaks the truth of the Scriptures."

Looking around, the former Bible teacher decides that those who feel the truth is on the side of the Rebaptizers are in the majority.

But Vadian has now finished his own little "book" against the Brothers, which he is to read the next morning before the Council. Conrad is right. The doctor's word will be the deciding factor in their judgment. The reading takes all day. The Brothers, sensing imminent defeat, appeal for equal time. It is granted, and a disputation follows. The Council deliberates. On Wednesday morning the people crowd back into the church for a public reading of the new mandate. The verdict is stern. No more special meetings in or outside the city will be tolerated. The Brothers, as a concession, may preach and read, but only at the precise hours when the official preaching is going on inside the church. Heavy fines will be levied against anyone

On Easter Sunday, 1525, over sixty persons in the south German city of Waldshut were baptized in the Anabaptist fellowship, including the Catholic priest Dr. Balthasar Hubmaier. In the days following, another 350 joined the Brothers. This mass departure from Catholic tradition caused the Austrians to occupy the town on December 5, 1525, and take away Waldshut's city rights as punishment for their unfaithfulness.

baptizing or being baptized, women as well as men. A force of 200 armed men will be sworn in to appear on short notice at City Hall to enforce the new rules.

Obviously, Conrad's anguished letter has failed to move Vadian. The movement has been outlawed in St. Gallen, and some of the aroused people have begun to do weird things under the pressure of the excitement. There are prophesyings, confessions, rumors, and finally a terrible nighttime murder by a religious crank, who runs to Vadian's house to confess. It all helps to convince Vadian that Ziwngli is right in his view of Baptizers as embittered fanatics.

If the movement is to catch fire afresh, the Brothers will have to try elsewhere. Conrad is eager to get back into the field, away from Zurich, where Zwingli's school for ministers will soon open and his sixteen-year-old sister Dorothea is about to have her marriage annulled. In these sad days an invitation has arrived for Conrad to visit the eminent Balthasar Hubmaier, who has been baptized at Waldshut with many of his congregation. Perhaps a new start can be made there. Conrad persuades a friend, Jacob Hottinger, to make the trip with him. Perhaps, as the young missionary once again leaves his hometown, he glances up at the clock of the new tower on the city wall, next to Froschauer's shop. He can not know, though it would not surprise him, that when he returns to Zurich in a few months, he will be led, not to Barbara and the children, but to a cell in that narrow stone fortress as a prisoner of the state.

Gruel, Bread & Water

Perched on a woody knoll, the tiny village of Grüningen resembles a ship, with the blunt bulwark of a castle as the prow. A tower at each end bears a streaming pennant, asserting to the peasants of this bailiwick on Lake Zurich the reigning authority of The Two Hundred of the City of Zurich, 25 miles to the northwest. The taller tower, thrusting up from the castle itself, serves as the district jail. Often, half his lifetime ago, young Conrad Grebel must have scrambled up the hill in its shadow, while his family had made the castle their home. Jacob, his father, had represented the power of Zurich, imposed now for many years on the area's peasants, as mayor from Conrad's second to his thirteenth year.

Thirteen years later, the current occupant of the castle, Jorg Berger, has his hands full. The ship of state in his territory, stretching from the eastern villages in the forested mountains south to the placid shores of Lake Zurich, is riding uneasily, its citizens near mutiny over their civil rights. The peasants (or "boors," as they have been unsympathetically called in their capital city) are filled with righteous indignation over the tax-and-tithe issue, and two months ago they vented their fury by sacking the local monastery. Conscientiously reporting every development to the Zurich Council, Magistrate Berger tries to keep the confidence of his neighbors by hearing their grievances. He knows that some of their pastors, especially those farthest from the city, such as Brennwald at Hinwil, are in sympathy with the resentment astir in the populace.

As the Grüningen peasants begin to mow the lush June meadows, a traveler arrives, intent on another kind of harvest. Conrad Grebel has come from Waldshut, where he has discussed the issue of baptism with Dr. Balthasar Hubmaier, and left the doctor determined to make a fresh try at persuading Zwingli that their teaching is the biblical one. By now Conrad, little more than a fugitive where once he was a son of the leading family, is filled with a blend of anger and sadness that he can find no fair hearing in his native city. The condemning tongue of Zwingli, once his brightest hope, now blocks every avenue of expression, branding Conrad as jealous and seditious. While the Reformer publishes book after book in mocking condemnation of the Brothers, they themselves have no access to the press or the pulpit, except as they can seize it on the run.

Conrad and Felix Mantz, in their disappointment and after looking at the New Testament with new eyes, have decided that a member of Christ's kingdom must withdraw from service in the civil government, since in that sphere people are, in the last analysis, forced by the power of the sword to conform to the laws. One must obey, whether one has repented or not. Conrad and Felix uphold this right of government to require civil obedience, but in the kingdom of God, they now preach, one lives a new kind of life not under compulsion, but in surrender of one's will to God's truth as it is shared in the community of believers. To require baptism under civil law, whereas Christ had called people to it in voluntary repentance, is to miss something of the very essence of the gospel, not a minor point. It is to reverse the whole process of freeing the church of Christ from bondage to the political process, which is an aspect of the human power struggle.

And the unbearable irony of the situation is that Conrad formerly heard Zwingli preach against this very tendency. "Take no sword in your hand but the Sword of the Spirit," Zwingli taught his followers less than three years ago. "As long as you cry out for the weapons of steel we will all see that you are not a disciple of Christ nor of Peter, but of the devil." Conrad, brawler that he once was, has found this teaching a great light, and he intends to walk in it. His change in this regard is remarkable. His friend Hubmaier, however, is less than convinced of this view. He believes that it is permissible for a Christian to fight in defense of his country, and to wield the power of the sword in civil office.

Perhaps such divergence of conviction has led Conrad to leave Waldshut for greener pastures in Grüningen. He discovers, traveling through the scenes of his boyhood, the barely controlled anger of the peasants toward the political and religious establishment in Zurich.

A model of the castle and town of Grüningen as it appeared in Conrad Grebel's day. The town is scarcely bigger now, but a new access road enters between the castle and the village.

Their grievances make them more ready to consider criticisms of Zwingli. Taking with him as preaching companion one of the first converts at Zollikon, a young vine-dresser Markus Bosshart, Conrad appears in Hinwil on a Sunday morning early in July and is pleased to see a large crowd gathering around for a sermon. They know what he is going to say — that there is no support for infant baptism in the Bible — and many already agree with him. After the sermon animated discussions break out. People are eager to hear the views of their former mayor's son, who is known to have been personally acquainted with Zwingli, and who has had disputes with him about infant baptism. When pastor Hans Brennwald himself arrives the discussion grows warm. Conrad says that if the pastor will read the Bible without prejudice, he will realize that he should wait to baptize the children of his parish until they have come to the age of reason.

"Milords of Zurich have issued a ruling on baptism," says Brennwald firmly, "and I intend to abide by it."

Conrad is disappointed. In other civil matters, where he is backed by the peasants' anger, Brennwald is contentious and bold enough. "You're quite the man," Conrad charges. "In a matter like this you shouldn't obey Milords or anybody else. What God tells us is what you should do."

The conversation veers toward the dictatorial attitude of Zurich's rulers. "It's a pity," Conrad complains, "that I am refused my rights in the matter of free expression, although I have appealed in the name of the empire, the state, and the faith." His confidence in the truth of his cause is so strong that he tells his fascinated listeners that he would be satisfied to be locked in jail, if only he then could have pen and ink, with the promise that the public would be able to read his opinions in his own words, instead of Zwingli's sarcastic interpretation. "I'll make a deal with him," argues Conrad. "Let us debate the question of baptism, using the Scripture as our only basis. If he proves me wrong, I'll agree to be burned to death as a heretic. And if I prove him wrong, I will not demand such a punishment for him."

Now the peasants have something new to discuss. As Conrad and Markus head for the nearby village of Bäretswil, where Conrad will preach this afternoon in a farmhouse, the gossip begins. One man claims that Conrad has heard Zwingli say brutally that the whole controversy of the tithes could be settled quickly if the magistrates would take three or four of the strongest opponents and chop off their heads. Pastor Brennwald, for his part, determines to begin keeping records in his parish immediately, to make sure that babies are baptized according to the Zurich law. Another peasant goes to his pastor and says, "If you had been at Hinwil today you'd have gotten your hat set straight."

"How so?" asks the pastor.

"Conrad Grebel was there and disputed with Pastor Brennwald on baptism and silenced him."

"If I had been there," responds the pastor, "I wouldn't have opposed him. There's no Scripture for it."

"And he preached on the Revelation of John."

"It takes more than an ordinary person to handle that," the pastor muses. But on further thought, he decides to go on baptizing infants, since it can't hurt them, and he cannot find explicit teaching against the practice in the Bible, any more than for it.

On Thursday, as they are staying in the home of a relative of Markus, an official messenger from Zurich finds Conrad and his companion and delivers to them a summons to appear at a hearing at the Council Hall in two days. They are charged with saying that Zwingli's new book on baptism is full of lies.

What shall they do? Markus is ready to head for Zurich, but Conrad senses danger. Though he would relish the chance for an open hearing, where he could at last express himself to the public of Zurich, he no longer trusts Zwingli. He decides to go only if the Council will grant them a prior promise of release when the hearing is over. While the messenger waits, he writes a reply asking that a guarantee of safe conduct be sent to the home of Rudi Thomann, one of the Brothers in Zollikon, where he and Markus can pick it up. "Insofar as we can serve you with obedience, our gracious Lords, in all temporal, dutiful affairs, we are ready to do so," Conrad writes. "Your faithful, obedient citizens and servants, Conrad Grebel and Markus Bosshart." Then, drawing a swift line below the signature, Conrad pours on the paper a bit of melted wax and presses his signet ring onto it. The rampant lion of the Grebel coat of arms, under the letters "C.G.," will assure the officials of Zurich that this is the authentic hand of the fugitive son of their colleague Jacob Grebel.

Saturday arrives, but a letter of safe conduct does not. Conrad feels that his caution has been justified, but Markus does not consider the situation dangerous, and goes to Zurich by himself. There, after a hearing, he is unceremoniously jailed. On the following day seven witnesses who have heard Conrad preach at Hinwil are carefully grilled for the evidence Zwingli wishes to find to support the charge that Conrad has been treasonously undermining the government.

And now a letter arrives for the lords of Zurich telling that another of their sons, Felix Mantz, has been preaching in fields and "causing discord" over baptism in Georg Blaurock's home territory of Chur. The local authorities have seized him, and are sending him home under guard, with the friendly request that he be kept there, so that Chur will not be forced to take stronger measures. When he is arraigned before the Zurich court, Felix explains in detail to the curious authorities how he and his friends escaped from the tower with blocks and a rope. He expresses the Brothers' wish that their views on baptism could be circulated in print, as Zwingli's are, and denies that he has ever said or taught that there should be no government or that people should not pay taxes or tithes. This charge, of course, is what Zwingli is eager to pin on him and Conrad and Georg Blaurock. When Felix is asked by what authority he preaches in the fields, he writes in his own hand in the court records, "Christ testified to His heavenly Father until death, and whoever testifies to the Father before men is Christ's disciple." Hearing this unyielding response, the court once again remands Felix to the jail tower in the Limmat.

Just a few months ago Zwingli wrote that "the Anabaptists make us difficulty only because of unimportant outward things, such as whether infants or adults should be baptized and whether a Christian may be an officer of the law." And it is true that when the hearings are held, little doctrinal discussion takes place. It is all about the nature of the church, and what behavior is required of a Christian, as well as belief. Zwingli is willing to assume that everyone in Zurich is, in some sense, a Christian. The Brothers have now come to conclude that such a "mass church" idea is alien to the New Testament. That is what makes the question of baptism so crucial, though no one has anticipated this. If the difference were only over what is discussed — but the Brothers insist on acting as if the kingdom of God were now fully present, not just a mental "believing." This kind of teaching is seen as a threat by the Catholic cantons, as well as Zurich. In Lucerne authorities seize one of Conrad's evangelizing converts. Learning that he began to baptize after reading an unprinted booklet that Conrad gave him, they burn him at the stake. Nevertheless the booklet, containing Scripture texts in support of the Brothers' position, is soon in print.

What keeps Zwingli increasingly tense is such pressure from the Catholic cantons. While Conrad is preaching in the fields of Grüningen, and Mayor Berger keeps filing reports on the Anabaptists with the Zurich Council, Zwingli feels that he must stabilize the situation. Forces of disorder dare not be permitted to flourish. Yet one night a gang of drunken soldiers makes a commotion in front of his house, challenging him to a fight. "Out with you, you red Ulrich! You thief, cowherd, seducer from Glarus!" Infuriated at Zwingli's opposition to their livelihood of mercenary soldiering, they smash his windows when he scorns their taunts. Such incidents only increase Zwingli's awareness that a tight rein must be kept.

He is happy to see the Council deciding to resist pressure from the rest of the Swiss cantons to tolerate the mass for the conservative people who still wish to attend it. But as he listens to their discussion he is deeply irritated to see old Jacob Grebel make an appeal for a compromise. He becomes suspicious that Jacob, whom he calls "a sorry jester" in a letter to Vadian, has the effect of endangering his Reformation by his calls for moderation. The son Conrad is too radical, and the father Jacob is too conservative. Zwingli, in his delicate political maneuvering, views them as a double threat.

When he hears a rumor that, even without Conrad, Felix, or Georg on the scene to stir things up, a surge of baptizing is again under way in Zollikon, he has a police force dispatched suddenly to make arrests. The rumor turns out to be false, and the Brothers who were apprehended are quickly released. But by now they are exhausted and intimidated. In a few weeks they decide, in conference, to give up baptizing and to obey the Council in this matter. It is the end of the new church in Zollikon; Zwingli will have rest from their zeal. Felix, in the tower, and Conrad, hiding in Grüningen, have lost part of their fellowship to the authority of Zurich, though the weakened Brothers do remain sympathetic to Conrad's cause.

In September Magistrate Berger reports an important catch to the Council: two men from Hubmaier's Anabaptist congregation at Waldshut, who have been helping Conrad Grebel to evangelize in Grüningen. After baptizing thirty persons, they have been seized, fined, and expelled. They do not carry weapons, like ordinary people. When they were arrested, the peasants of Grüningen defended them. Because of this unpredictably rebellious spirit, Berger has felt for some time that the officials of Zurich should allow a public discussion with the Anabaptists, so that his people will not keep complaining about unfair suppression.

The second Sunday of October turns out to be a remarkable day not only for Mayor Berger, but for Georg Blaurock, Conrad, and even Felix Mantz, who has just been released from the jail tower in the Limmat the day before. He had to promise not to baptize, but by next morning has found Conrad in Grüningen, and goes with him to an open-air meeting. Meanwhile, Berger hears a report that a man in a blue coat, with black hair and a bald spot, has boisterously taken over the pulpit in the Hinwil church by arriving before Pastor Brennwald. Berger's deputy mayor, who was present, has hurriedly ridden to find his superior, and told him that the stranger announced, "If this is the place to proclaim God's Word, I am sent here by the Father to proclaim it!" Berger gallops to Hinwil with the deputy, where they find the church filled with 200 people listening to Georg Blaurock. As they begin to leave the building, Berger enjoins them by an oath of loyalty to do their civil duty and help to arrest Georg. No one will cooperate. It is left to Berger, his deputy, and a servant to seize Georg, set him on a horse and lead him toward Grüningen castle. Young and old, the congregation crowds around, and Georg bursts into a song as he jogs along. The people begin clamoring for a sermon. When it seems that they will begin an unlawful assembly in a circle around the magistrate, he begs them not to cause trouble.

And now to Berger's utter astonishment, here come Conrad Grebel and Felix Mantz, intending to hold an open meeting of their own to the gospel. Quickly changing his strategy, Berger rides to the next town to gather reinforcements, sends them to arrest Grebel and

Mantz, and guides Blaurock on toward Grüningen castle. By night-fall there are two prize Anabaptists in the tower: Conrad and Georg. Felix, only a day out of the Zurich jail, has slipped away in the confusion.

As Berger sits down that evening in what was once Conrad Grebel's home to write an immediate report of the momentous captures to his lords in Zurich, a few feet away, behind an impenetrable stone wall, Conrad is adjusting his weary bones to the dungeon. Perhaps, before he falls asleep, the clinking of cowbells from the meadows sloping away from the castle wall carries his memory back to the July evenings of his boyhood. Then he represented the power of the canton's lords. But now the powers-that-be count him their enemy. Conrad knows that many of the people in Grüningen are extremely sympathetic to his preaching, and he wonders what their reaction will be if he is removed from their jurisdiction into a court of Zurich. In the darkness of the tower, he ponders the conflict between the kingdom of God and the civil structures of this world.

As for Zwingli, the news strikes him as heartening. By Wednesday he writes to Vadian, "Conrad Grebel has been caught and lies in jail in Grüningen along with that wild fellow, Georg. With his tendency to bad luck, he always seemed to expect some tragedy. Now he has achieved it. May the great God grant that his Word will suffer no damage." Then he drops a dark hint of his displeasure with Jacob Grebel, who has doubtless already tried to suggest moderation in the treatment of his obstreperous son. Zwingli has finished playing with Conrad.

Zurich now demands of its subjects in Grüningen that they bring the prisoners to town for trial. The peasants are extremely reluctant to comply, and appeal for an open disputation on the tormented subject of baptism. A letter with a similar burden arrives in Zurich from the weary Brothers of Zollikon. The request is warily granted, and three days are set aside for one more debate. Felix Mantz, who has been seized again, as well as several other Anabaptists, including Michael Sattler, former monastery prior from north of the Rhine, will be brought there. The main speakers for the Anabaptists will be Conrad, Felix, and Georg, opposing Zwingli and the other two city preachers.

On Monday, November 6, after considerable publicity, an im-

mense crowd gathers in the Council Hall on the Limmat. The three
Anabaptist "ringleaders" are brought from the New Tower on the
city wall, but the press is so great that the debate must be re-
convened in the cavernous nave of the Great Church. On hand as
two of the designated chairmen are Vadian, and Dr. Hofmeister, in
whose home in Schaffhausen Conrad so hopefully debated last January. But now Hofmeister, the new pastor of Our Lady's Church in
Zurich, has taken Zwingli's side of the matter. Twelve neutral ob-
servers from Grüningen are present to make sure that the Brothers
are given adequate chance to express themselves without intimidation
and interruption. Zwingli sets forth three propositions which are to
be defended or refuted:

1. Christian children are no less God's children than their parents, as in
   the Old Testament Israel.

2. Circumcision is the old form of what baptism is to us; we still give
   the sign of the covenant to children.

3. There is no teaching or example of rebaptism in God's Word. When
   people are rebaptized, Christ is crucified afresh.

While we have no way of listening to this debate as it drags
on for the three days, we can imagine the Brothers quoting many
Scriptures, Conrad reminding Zwingli of his earlier statements which
got Conrad "into this thing" in the first place, and Georg using
the sharpest language, even calling Zwingli a thief and a robber, as
the Reformer had once called false priests in a sermon on the tenth
chapter of John. At last Conrad is having his say in public, before
nearly a thousand listeners, in the bare-walled Great Church. But as
the closing hour arrives the Council with utter predictability declares that the Anabaptists' teachings have been discredited.

Now that the debate is dismissed, a regular trial begins at once.
Testimony flows in from Zwingli, Dr. Hofmeister, Pastor Brennwald
of Hinwil, and others, regarding what the Anabaptists have said.
Again and agan they are accused of fomenting sedition. Conrad denies that he has ever taught people to disobey the government. He
admits that he thinks infant baptism is of the devil, not God, and
that Zwingli therefore teaches falsehood. He has never maintained
that a Christian may have no private property, but he does

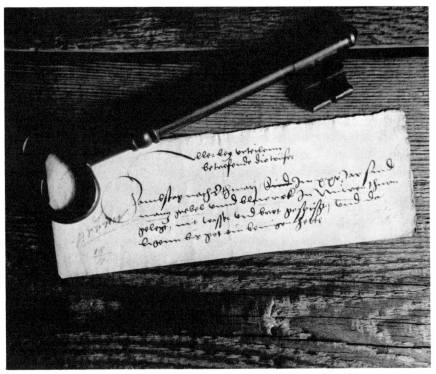

This notice of imprisonment records that on a certain Saturday Mantz, Blaurock, and Grebel were placed in the New Tower on the Zurich city wall, put on water and bread, and imprisoned indefinitely.

claim the necessity of excluding people from the church who live immorally. He has never told Zwingli that he shouldn't preach a doctrine until he has talked it over with the Brothers. What he did say in Leo Jud's house was that if a person wants to preach, he should preach nothing but the Word of God. He denies having claimed special revelations, though his friend Georg Blaurock has spoken to him of such experiences. He denies having accused Zwingli of adultery. And regarding baptism he believes that the two other city pastors, Leo Jud and Caspar Megander, know very well, if they would admit it, that no one should baptize infants.

But even such moderate testimony is enough to condemn Conrad, Felix, and Georg. Three of their friends, including Michael Sattler "with the white cape," are expelled from the canton. They themselves are dumped back into the gruesome New Tower on the city wall, to dine on gruel, bread, and water as long as God and Milords see fit. No one but the keeper is to see them. To prevent further outbreaks of their teaching, a strict new law is about to be passed by the Council expressly forbidding rebaptism in Grüningen territory.

As the damp chill of the tower closes in once more on Conrad's aching joints, we may imagine him at the lowest point in his life. His brother-in-law Vadian, on the other hand, has reached the top. He is about to be elected mayor of his hometown, St. Gallen. But Conrad remains strong in his commitment. Eventually Felix manages to have candles smuggled into the tower, and there is opportunity to write and exhort each other not to weaken. Some books are there which they strain to read in the dim light. A minority Bible college is going on here in the gloom, at the same time that Zwingli meets in morning sessions with the Hebrew students of the Great Church. Conrad has time to write down his arguments for voluntary baptism. And doubtless there are surreptitious visits from sympathetic Brothers. Henry Aberli, Conrad's old baker friend from Raceway Street, brings the comfort of fresh bread, and the Lord's Supper can be eaten even here.

During these dark months Dr. Hubmaier comes to Zurich, hoping to help the cause of the Brothers. In four days he too is arrested, required to explain his views before four preachers, and when Zwingli finds his ideas erroneous, thrown into jail and tortured.

Three times, reports Zwingli, he cries out his admission of error, while miserably stretched on the rack. A week later he lets his retraction be made public, with the astonishing explanation that Zwingli and Conrad's old schoolteacher friend Myconius have persuaded him to let love be the rule, and not cling so stubbornly to his own idea. After several more weeks Zwingli takes him to a Sunday service in Our Lady's Church, has the retraction read, and preaches a sermon to close the matter. Suddenly Hubmaier charges up into the pulpit like Georg Blaurock and begins to defend adult baptism, declaring that his retraction was secured by torture. Zwingli in his disappointment has him thrown back into the jail tower in the Limmat, where the dreary trial enters another cycle.

It is now March of 1525, three and one-half months since Conrad, Georg, and Felix have received their indefinite sentence. Letters reporting Anabaptist activities in Grüningen are steadily carried to Zurich from the harried Mayor Berger. Finally the Council decides it must make an example of the imprisoned leaders and a dozen of their followers. A hearing is held. Summoned from their dreary quarters, Conrad, Felix, and Georg stand rock-firm in the court. The clerk writes in his record:

> Conrad Grebel answers that infant baptism is not right, and that the baptism which he has accepted is right. He wishes to abide by this and let God in control. In all other worldly matters he wishes to be obedient to Milords. He wishes to declare that Zwingli is mistaken in this and other matters, and he petitions Milords that they will allow him to write publicly, as Zwingli does. If this may not be, he hopes to bear his lot as God wills.

The transcript of this unyielding testimony is read before the Council for a decision. In the deliberation, Jacob Grebel suggests mercy while Zwingli fumes.

In two days they have prepared a sentence. Conrad, Felix, and Georg with nine other men and six women shall lie together in the New Tower, fed only bread and water, and bedded on straw, until death. The guard must give his oath not to let anyone visit them, even if they are sick. The women, married and unmarried, shall have the same treatment as the men. A public decree shall be released to announce the severe sentence. Anyone who baptizes again will be paid back in kind by drowning without mercy.

"At last," writes Zwingli to Vadian within a few hours of the decision, our tortured patience has been exhausted. "I am extremely displeased at the audacity some men have." Vadian recognizes that Zwingli is referring to Conrad's father. Doubtless his own feelings are more in line with another letter arriving a few days later, in which one of his former students in Vienna and a close friend of Conrad's writes, "Our poor Conrad . . . is condemned to perpetual imprisonment unless he recants." Knowing his brother-in-law as he does, the burgomaster of St. Gallen can hardly expect such a solution. As for Jacob Grebel, he now has a daughter in the mayor's house of St. Gallen, and a son in the dungeon of Zurich.

Sudden, Sorrowful News

Two weeks after Zurich's lords have passed the sentence of life imprisonment on their Anabaptist prisoners, a night of excitement unfolds at the New Tower on the city wall by the cemetery of the Dominican Cloister. It is Wednesday evening, and the guard hands in some water, which the prisoners share with a little bread. The weather is damp and cold; one of the men is too sick to join the conversation. Suddenly someone notices that the shutter on a window above them is unaccountably standing open. The discovery makes them catch their breath in anticipation. But Conrad, Felix, and Georg say that they will not try to escape. They will die in the tower. Yet, after several of them lift each other up, and make a pile of wooden blocks and books, Felix clambers up too. Four of them, now on the wall, call down that everything is open for a fairly easy escape. They let each other down with the rope and ratchet used to bring them in, and stand together in the dry moat while the last one slithers down the rope by himself.

Now what? One man, a tailor, standing there in the rain, announces that he is going to get his tailor's equipment and go to work in a town by Lake Zurich. Someone jokes, "Let's go to the red Indians across the ocean!" They cross the strangely lowered drawbridge and knock at the gate. By coincidence or providence the watchman is a brother of one of the escapees. He takes several of them in, giving his wife a great scare, and prepares to serve them bread, cheese, and drink. Suddenly a constable stops to check into the commotion, and takes them right back into the hands of the law.

And what of Conrad? He has vanished into the murky night. Zurich has seen the last of its native son.

Had someone left the window open purposely? We shall never know. We catch only a quick glimpse of Conrad heading north once

137

again, traveling with one of the men from Waldshut who helped him preach and baptize in Grüningen last summer. As they pass through the villages on the road to the Rhine, Ulrich Teck asks Conrad where he is planning to go. Conrad replies, "I don't want to say." And indeed, when Ulrich is taken once more before the Zurich Council in a few weeks, he cannot divulge what he does not know.

Zwingli, though, "knows" what motivates Conrad. "However he may deny it," he writes to a friend, Conrad "has turned against his parents for no other reason than that they have refused to give him everything his arrogance demands." But then Zwingli "knows" some dubious things. He knows that Hubmaier is wrong about baptism, and requires him now to recant publicly in three churches, before being allowed out of town secretly. He "knows" that Jacob Grebel secretly conspires to block the Reform.

We can well understand Zwingli's hair-trigger nervousness. Later in the spring a man gallops his horse uproariously down the aisle of the Great Church, calling out that Zwingli is a rogue, thief, heretic, traitor, and soul-murderer. "My opponents in Zurich," Zwingli comments grimly, "are cooperating with my enemies throughout the Confederation." Still, he presses forward boldly with his Reform program, and has a compulsory baptismal register set up as part of the civil takeover of the old Catholic system.

In May and June, while Conrad preaches in distant townships, Zwingli suffers the severest blow his hopes for a reformed Switzerland have yet received. A debate has been called between Reformers and Catholics up the Limmat in Baden. John Eck, Luther's famous opponent, will argue the Catholic side, while two Reformers — one from Bern and one from Basel — will defend Zwingli's teachings. The preacher of Zurich, whose hopes for a great national movement ride on the outcome, is offered a safe passage, but he quips in refusal, "I do not wish to bathe in Baden." His fear of the Catholics is all too real. He has received too many threats. For weeks he gets little or no sleep as the great dispute rages, fueled by ideas he keeps smuggling daily to the Protestant speakers. At last the discussion closes and the votes are counted. Eighty-two to ten in favor of the Catholic side! The Reform has stalled. It will not, apparently, sweep through the Swiss Confederation with Zwingli as its Moses-leader! It is even in danger of being suppressed where it has officially taken root. Zwingli's back is to the wall. It is well for Conrad that he is nowhere near Zurich.

In spite of the Reformer's growing, almost compulsive, suspicions of Jacob Grebel's loyalty, the aging guild master, is still selected by the Council for weighty and delicate political assignments. Now he is on a committee to place the staff of the Great Church directly under the administration of the Council. With his three grandchildren living fatherless with the unhappy Barbara, and with the necessity of forcing an angry cousin, Peter Grebel, a conservative member of the Great Church staff, to resign, his relations with his clan are hardly pleasant. Young Dorothea has remarried, this time to another of Conrad's old friends, an acceptable aristocrat. Transcending family affairs, however, Jacob, with his stately air and his snowy mane and beard, remains one of Zurich's respected and trusted citizens.

Does he brood over his only living son, Conrad? Does he hear reports that a booklet from Conrad's pen on the subject of baptism has been printed and is circulating, to Zwingli's disgust? Does he have hopes that the frail young scion of the Grebel clan will yet find a niche in the city on the Limmat, once the tumult of change gives way to a happy equilibrium? Does Barbara, with her three children, the oldest hardly four years old, pine for her stern young missionary husband? Does Vadian anticipate an eventual reconciliation with the brother-in-law he has loved?

Whatever their thoughts, there arrives in the city of Zurich, in the summer of 1526, sudden and sorrowful news. In the city of Maienfeld, just east of the Rhine near the distant home of Georg Blaurock, the fragile body of Conrad Grebel, abused by a winter in the tower of his native Zurich, has been broken at last by the plague. There, perhaps in the home of his sister Barbara, the pest has struck down one whom it has so often spared before. History allows us no access to the bedside of this servant of Christ who has not reached the age of thirty, nor can we hear any parting words. We can only return to the city which bore this failed student, eager evangelist, and indignant outcast.

There we see a jubilant celebration of the joining of St. Gallen with Zurich in the Reformation. A festive procession winds up to the Lindenhof, where a banquet is prepared for 700. The guest of honor

Grebel lived scarcely a year after the beginning of the believers' church in Zurich and Zollikon. His general poor health and the fatigue of living as a fugitive combined to make him more susceptible to the plague. Grebel died in July or August, 1526, in this town of Maienfeld, possibly in the home of his sister, Barbara.

is Vadian, chief citizen of St. Gallen. Afterward, many hundreds of Zurich's citizens join their visitors in trooping through the narrow streets of the city on the Limmat to acclaim the new accord. Jacob Grebel, father-in-law of the distinguished visiting dignitary, is at the zenith of his social standing.

What happens to him a few months later, then, is almost beyond belief. The name of his son Conrad, who has been dead for months, is again mentioned in the Council Hall, and his university days in Vienna and Paris are recalled. Dignified Jacob Grebel stands in sad amazement as he hears a blizzard of accusations that he himself is, of all things, a treasonous enemy of the state of Zurich. Having for decades driven himself through the pains of gout and the loss of business to represent the interests of the city in every imaginable political affair, he now stands poisonously accused by Ulrich Zwingli himself of having, with others, accepted foreign pensions contrary to the laws of the canton. What possesses Zwingli? Is the state really so threatened that a moderate senator in his sixties must be punished to intimidate others? In consternation, Jacob sees that his record has been carefully researched, old gossip rehashed, and Zwingli, who once called Conrad arrogant for demanding money from his father, now accuses the father of desperate stinginess. To the rack he must go, where the aged body is twisted to force him to change his story. But he calmly sticks to it; he claims innocence. Perhaps Conrad did receive money from the Pope's representative. Perhaps Jacob had said, half-jokingly, "Go see the Pope's man." But he had done nothing treasonous, and besides, that was several years ago, not long after Zwingli himself had stopped taking a pension from the Pope.

No one yet dreams how deep Zwingli's anger runs toward the man he feels slows the Reformation, how airtight a case he has built, how carefully he will pull political strings. Even Myconius the schoolmaster, to whom Conrad had complained so bitterly from Paris, steps forward to give testimony for the prosecution. But surely Jacob is in no danger of severe punishment? Why, only last month the Council once again commissioned him with two other men to reconcile a nearby monastery with the dissident local peasants. Yet the tension is high; there is an ominous note in the air. Another man similarly accused by Zwingli takes the chance to escape from the city hidden in a manure cart.

Suddenly, in the early afternoon of October 30, Jacob's trial comes to an end. The sentence of the Council is read like a thunderclap. Jacob Grebel is to be beheaded for high treason! There is a strange rush to carry out the sentence. Unable to believe what is happening, Senator Grebel is led to the Fish Market at the Limmat, proclaiming that he deserves no such punishment. But within an hour of the sentencing the astonished witnesses on the bridge watch the bearded white head of Zurich's trusted servant tumble in blood to the ground.

A wave of dismay spreads from the Fish Market over the city, and beyond, but no one in the tense Reformed city dares raise a public protest. Some citizens opine quietly that this is Zwingli's frustrated revenge on Conrad, the son. Other theories are gossiped about. Many feel that if the execution had not been carried out so rapidly nothing would have come of the whole affair. In corroboration of this belief, other men who were accused with Jacob Grebel of the same crimes are allowed back in Zurich and reinstated in their places. Vadian, recoiling in shock from "that disgraceful affair," confides that he dare not give way to "the ocean of my feelings."

Zwingli, however, is gratified. He writes to a friend that he has discovered that Jacob was even worse as a man than he had realized: "When the widow of Conrad, who died a few months ago, asked her father-in-law for her inheritance (which usually amounts to one third) she was rebuffed with the statement that Conrad had left no money." And, solidifying his position, Zwingli notes with satisfaction the passing of a new law by the Council imposing the death penalty on anyone rebaptizing or even attending Anabaptist preaching. The church of Christ must and will be protected from fanatics. A program of suppression is now under way.

The first victim, seized within a few weeks, is well known to us. Jorg Berger, the exasperated mayor of Grüningen, surprises Felix Mantz and Georg Blaurock with two other Anabaptists at a secret meeting, and brings them to Zurich, where they are put in quarters they know all too well — the jail tower in the Limmat. Zwingli now holds all the cards. The drama has nearly played itself out.

On Saturday, January 5, 1527, the familiar dreadful story is reenacted. Because Conrad Grebel's friend Felix has become involved in Anabaptism, has become a leader and teacher of such things, because he separated himself from the Christian church, because he condemned capital punishment and boasted of revelations from Paul's letters, and because such teachings lead to offense and revolt, and the breaking up of brotherly love and civil harmony, he must be executed by drowning, and his property confiscated by Milords. The constables fetch him from the jail tower by boat, and take him to the fishers' hut in the middle of the Limmat just beyond the bridge at the Council Hall. There, as he refuses the persistent plea of a minister to recant and hears encouraging shouts from his mother and brothers on the bank, the city servants of the Christian city of Zurich tie his hands together, strip them over his knees, and push a stick through the crook. Felix sings in Latin, "Father, into Thy hands I commend my spirit," and, bent awkwardly in his bonds, he is thrust beneath the swift green current to drink his death.

Having thus advanced the cause of brotherly love, the constables turn next to Georg Blaurock, the last of the three main Anabaptist leaders. Since he is not a native of Zurich, he will leave the town alive, but not without a memorable lesson in civil peace. His upper garments are stripped off, and he is chased panting down the long Lower Village Street, whacked with rods until the blood streams down, and his life, as Zwingli notes wryly, is seriously endangered. At the city gate the beating stops, but Georg is requested to take an oath never to return. "I can't," he says defiantly. "God has forbidden it." Driven back to the tower to await the Council's further action, he reconsiders and consents to take the oath. But at the gate he solemnly shakes the dust from his shoes and his clothes in token of God's judgment.

Georg has two and one-half years to preach the kingdom of God before he will give his life in flames for the witness. By then Michael Sattler, "the brother in the white coat," writer of the first statement of the Brothers' beliefs, will have suffered the same martyrdom, as will Dr. Hubmaier, a prolific Anabaptist writer, in Catholic Austria. Europe is not yet ready for their testimony, any more than Jerusalem was for Christ's.

As for Barbara, a year and a half after Conrad's death, she marries a Jacob Ziegler. Conrad's and Barbara's youngest son, Joshua, will grow up to have a son Conrad too, who will, as a member of Zurich's state church, serve as treasurer of the city that spurned his grandfather of the same name. And this treasurer's grandson, also named Conrad Grebel, will one day be burgomaster of Zurich. Still more — in an irony of history — the pastor of the Great Church itself, where Conrad Grebel was kindled to the gospel of Christ by Ulrich Zwingli, is, as these words are written four and one-half centuries later, the direct descendant, in the thirteenth generation, of the Conrad we have known.

Ulrich Zwingli, despondent after years of difficult efforts to reform Switzerland, dies five years after Conrad on the battlefield of a Swiss civil war he has helped to provoke. Sprawled with him on the field are the bodies of 24 other Christian chaplains from Zurich, one of the pastors Georg Blaurock has interrupted, a fellow student of Conrad Grebel's in Vadian's classes at Vienna, and three former Anabaptists from Zollikon, won back to Zwingli's cause.

When the news of the Protestant defeat and Zwingli's death arrives in St. Gallen, the 47-year-old burgomaster slumps in despair. But he lives on modestly, ever the scholar as well as the home-loving politician, for another twenty years. Making a gift of his considerable library to the city, he includes a bulging heap of letters he has collected over the years, containing some fifty in the round script of the young brother-in-law for whom he had once hoped so much. In the library of St. Gallen, jealously guarded from thief and decay, with ancient manuscripts saved from the town's monastery, one may yet read the outpourings of Conrad's young soul — his bright literary hopes, his youthful despair, his love, and his testimony to the new light that shone from the Word of God across the decaying parapets and ceremonies of Europe.

Myconius, companion on the mountain-climbing journey on which we first made Conrad's acquaintance, is now the head pastor in the city of Basel, and a stern opponent of the Anabaptists. Glarean, the temperamental teacher in Paris, has won fame as a Catholic humanist professor at Freiburg, with Erasmus, and together they scorn Zwingli's movement. To these men, as to Vadian, Conrad Grebel has been a disappointment. Yet in his unfulfilled promise, the intensity of his ardor, the totalness of his reckless loyalty to Christ, he will be to many a fellow seeker of the kingdom what Vadian affectionately calls him years after the passionate young voice has been stilled: "My Conrad Grebel."

When the call of Jesus Christ was heard inviting citizens of earthly empires to enter the kingdom of God, our Conrad Grebel rose up and followed.

A Meditation

In the cracked and mottled mirror of history, the features of Conrad Grebel's intense young face are not as clearly focused as we would like. The intimate confessions of his letters flicker briefly amid obscuring shadows. Yet his passionate implication in the struggle of the Swiss Christian church to cast off the pagan corrosions of centuries makes it difficult to ignore him and the questions he raised. Millions of Christians around the world now accept as obvious what Conrad and his Brothers were once scorned for demanding: the freedom of Christ's church from state control.

In the generations since Conrad's untimely death, it has more often than not been his misfortune to have his career explained to the public by people who have not shared his commitments, or by those who find in the topic of his unrounded, testy temperament a handy extenuation of Ulrich Zwingli's disturbing harshness. Unfavorable reactions are to be expected from those who, like Zwingli, assume that any decision like Conrad's to identify with a believing, disciplined "few" rather than a corporately "Christian Zurich" must be wrong-headedly "sectarian." But a further fogging of his historical image occurs when his admirers confer on his conversion the vocabulary of the particular pieties of our own post-Anabaptist era, and, this safely established, regale each other with speculations on his fairly conventional escapades year as a student playboy in Paris. Our current concerns and theses may thus emerge more crisply, as we peer back into sixteenth-century Zurich, than the personalities and confrontations we attempt to depict.

We need neither whitewash nor magnify Conrad's querulousness, however, if we focus on issues that transcend the dynamics of his personal psyche. If, after all, it is merely human interest we hunt, the soul of Ulrich Zwingli offers a richer complexity, more bountiful gifts, vaster political consequence. We are driven back to seek out Conrad, rather, because the new fellowship in which he was a primary participant proclaimed truth that refuses to die, for all its inconvenience, and that flares more brightly with the unfolding of human history.

Like Isaac Newton, Zwingli proposed the brilliant answers of a genius to basic questions, while considering marginal unsolved areas as negligible in relation to the larger truths. But, building from Newton's apparently small discrepancies, Albert Einstein has shown that, for all his intelligence, Newton's model of the cosmos works only within no longer tenable assumptions. The annoyingly minor discrepancies are actually crucial. Although Conrad Grebel is not a "great mind," he made an analogous determination with his band of outcast Christian brothers, and risked his life to affirm its truth. What the Western Christian establishment has so often regarded as the marginal issue of "social tactics" (as opposed to "doctrine") is not only inextricable from the faith, but the very arena in which the meaning of Christ's cross — the criterion of the faith — becomes clear.

Conrad found, in the months after his conversion, that a theory of the cross as threatening one of two contending political parties and supporting the other did not square with the New Testament or with Christian experience. The cross undermines *both* parties — it is the repudiation of the conventional power struggle. Yet, while claiming the cross as their sign, both Zwingli's Protestant friends and his Catholic foes briskly executed whatever Anabaptists they could find. They were unable, apparently, to recognize any important distinction between violent fomenters and those who had inexplicably forsworn the sword.

Caught in that ancient crossfire, it was Conrad's lot to think the unthinkable; to renounce Zwingli's optimism regarding eventual human willingness to obey the truth when it is proclaimed; to learn the stimultaneously dark and joyous logic of Christ's cross, and to take it as his only security. That his rediscovery is often trivialized by prepared stereotypes is only evidence that the issues on which he and Zwingli differed are alive in human loyalties today.

ENVISION, now, a traveler from a North American Mennonite family meditating among the monuments of Switzerland, four and one-half centuries after Conrad Grebel risked his Helvetian citzenship for a heavenly one. This particular pilgrim counts among his physical ancestors the Altdörfers of Kloten, farmers of the Grebels' ancestral estate north of Zurich, and the stubborn Landeses along Lake Zurich, last of the Swiss Anabaptist families to surrender a martyr to the executioners of Zurich's Christian government. The modern visitor has been nurtured, let us note, in the lap of a sequestered community of farmers by Pennsylvania hills far gentler than the stunning Alps of their forebears. In one of their humble, unsteepled meetinghouses he has been baptized into a fellowship that traces directly back to the gathering in the home of Felix Mantz at which Conrad Grebel poured the water of a new life in Christ on the head of Georg Bluecoat. By now the traveler has been joined in that fellowship by thousands from all races and cities. The water of this baptism is thicker than the tribal blood of the Swiss.

As the cable car on Mt. Pilatus wafts him and his fellow passengers far above lucent Lucerne, the pilgrim imagines Conrad and Vadian below him laboring up through the flowering slopes toward the lake which has long since dried away. Again, at Grüningen, he is touched when the little blond boy, whose family now lives in the castle where Conrad grew up, reports innocently that his name is Felix.

A day later, high on a hillside meadow above St. Gallen, the pilgrim pauses to trace, in the street pattern below, the curving walls of the ancient monastery, on whose site rises a cathedral built long since the passing of its most famous citizen, Burgomaster Vadian. The doctor has not yet been forgotten here. The pilgrim finds a Vadian Street here and a Zwingli Street there. A brown stone statue of Conrad's mild brother-in-law holding a large book stands massively where the newer city begins, looking back toward the monastery. The cathedral itself flaunts a fantastically lavish display of baroque gold, ironically crowned above the chancel with the words in Latin, "Blessed are the poor in spirit." As the pilgrim watches, two devout women walk up to an image of the dead Christ, solemnly caress the shiny body, cross themselves, and depart. Following them, the pilgrim finds no Grebel Street, but a friendly librarian in the town archives brings to the reading room several of the letters Vadian saved. The visitor is embarrassed to have one of

Conrad's wax seals come off its letter in his hands, after centuries of faithful adherence. "May the faith not similarly die through my carelessness, having lived until this generation," is his prayer.

Arriving at Einsiedeln, the pilgrim finds himself unprepared for the munificence of the shrine where Zwingli preached before his call to Zurich. Busloads of the faithful fan out over the vast cobblestoned square before the huge twin-towered sanctuary, buying candles and religious trinkets. For all Zwingli's thunderings in nearby Zurich, the canton of Schwyz is as Catholic as ever, and even the candle of Zurich is carried yearly in procession to burn before the statue of the Virgin, now considered more miraculous than ever, having been turned a lustrous black by the smoke of countless tapers consuming themselves in her sanctified presence.

And now, following Zwingli's next move, the traveler speeds along the highway on the southern shore of Lake Zurich, toward the upper end of the city bisected by the beginning Limmat. Walls and the jail tower in the Limmat have disappeared, but the double spires of the Great Church, rounded off by architects in a recent century, still beckon. Where frogs once croaked in the moat by the southern wall now teems the traffic of the world's wealthiest street. The business of Zurich is banking. Leafy limes still crown the Lindenhof, from which the pilgrim surveys the towers of St. Peter's and Our Lady's Church on this side of the river, and those of the Dominican Monastery and the Great Church on the other. Now for many years attached at one end to the encroaching quay, the Water Church stands with its other skirts in the Limmat, site of the ancient islet where the Celts once practiced their cult. Behind it, the pilgrim notes on his map, is the statue of Zwingli, which he will need to visit. And just at the foot of the old Roman hill is the spot in the Limmat where Felix Mantz was drowned.

In the great national museum nearby the traveler comes upon a painting of Zurich done in Conrad's childhood for an altarpiece in the Great Church. Alien as he finds the thought of images in worship, the pilgrim is yet saddened to observe that this marvelously colorful likeness of the city has been cut by irreverent hands to a smaller size, leaving only the heads and shoulders of the city saints, Felix, Regula, and a later addition, Exuperantius, sorrowfully visible as they undergo their legendary martyrdom by the Limmat. Behind them, in a glory of red-tiled roofs, Conrad Grebel's Zurich plies its crafts and points its spires toward heaven. And in another room the pilgrim is startled to read the announcement beside a glass-enclosed, glistening helmet and sword, that these were taken from the body of Ulrich Zwingli when he fell in the battle of Kappel.

Walking across the bridge and up into New Market Street, the pilgrim finds the Grebel home, now, in the latest of several mutations, with a quiet restaurant on its first floor, bearing the name "Harmony." Once inside he is astounded by a note on the menu informing him that it was from this very house that V. I. Lenin departed from his stay in Zurich, on his fateful journey to the Finland Station in Leningrad, fifty years ago, carrying the atheistic gospel of communism. How startling that from one dwelling should have issued both the man who had inaugurated the fellowship in which he had heard the call of Christ, and the one who launched the most massive attack on religion in history! The pilgrim leaves in a daze at the discovery.

Now dusk falls, and the ancient hillside alleys fill with noisy pleasure-seekers strolling toward cafes and theaters. The pilgrim approaches the Great Church Square, passes Zwingli's office, and notes the narrow New City Street climbing in a cobblestoned angle toward the home of Felix Mantz. The strains of a choir concert call him into the church itself, past the bulletin board where the name of the pastor is announced: Hans Rudolph von Grebel. What a plain church! Astonishingly austere and bare! The difference Zwingli made is overwhelming, especially when one compares these unadorned walls with the golden splender of Einsiedeln. What energy must have been released to cast out the images! And there at that pulpit, while images still spangled the walls, was trumpeted the life-giving Word of Christ that awakened Conrad Grebel, son of Zurich, and — after centuries — the visiting pilgrim, who suddenly bows his head and prays.

Here, he reflects, is where so much that he lives by was first proclaimed, later to be clarified and refined in the fires of persecution. Baptism deliberately and joyfully accepted as the beginning of a new life, the Lord's Supper as an expression of brotherhood, abandonment of hopelessly rooted human violence, the freeing of the church from all loyalties but the Rule of Christ, making this Rule

151

the required norm of discipline — all this which had become tradition in Pennsylvania and was again in danger of being lost was once new here in Zurich. It was then a spark of discovery jumping between the lips of Ulrich Zwingli and the mind of young Conrad Grebel. Here is where it must first have been borne in upon Conrad that "human judgment" and "the custom of the fathers" of Zurich or any city will not stand before the inbreaking of the divine Word of grace. He leaped angrily into the kingdom of God, muses the pilgrim, but threw away his earthly sword.

And now, finally, to walk behind the Water Church and look up at the spotlighted statue of Zwingli. There the great leader clasps his arm under a Bible holding in a decisive grasp beneath it the hilt of his downward-pointing sword. He stands at the spot where he landed when coming by boat from Einsiedeln to bring the gospel to Zurich, while Conrad was a lonely student in Paris. He had come to free the church from pagan customs lurking everywhere under a layer of Christian symbol.

The pilgrim's eyes are drawn again and again to the dark sword of the statue. Just here — on this very spot when it was an island in the Limmat — it had been storied for centuries that a sword had once been put to the necks of Felix and Regula, the saints of Zurich. Sad, but such was the price of breaking with the entrenched pagan rites formerly conducted at this place of worship. By the blood of these martyrs light had broken forth to the Helvetians, the light of the true God, whose own Son had likewise laid down His life to the force of a Roman regime allied with a Hebrew priesthood. And yet when Zwingli landed at this same holy place more than a millennium later, it was with burning conviction that in many ways Zurich, Switzerland, Europe had never fully put on the new life in Christ. They might commemorate the martyrs, but their own history continued to be stained by blood and greed, and the crosses above their altars had presided over, rather than interrupted, the inveterate ritual of rivalry.

Zwingli's powerful lips had announced the reviving of the gospel in the midst of the years, and Conrad Grebel, one of Zurich's promising sons, had heard the call and gone over to the new life described in the old, unread Book. Having abandoned the sword of his secular citizenship, Conrad looked behind only to see, in dismay,

Zwingli's statue behind the Water Church on the Limmat. Clutching both the sword and the Scriptures, Zwingli chose to continue the Constantinian synthesis of church and state, the "Christian nation" concept challenged by the Anabaptists.

one still clutched in the hand of his teacher Zwingli, shortly to be waved menacingly in his direction. And only a few paces downstream from where Zurich's original Christian martyrdom was thought to have transpired, Zwingli himself was party to the martyrdom of others in the name of Christ's church. The statue faces away from the site of Felix Mantz's drowning, as if in perplexity, and toward Zwingli's eastward home in the Toggenburg and the shrine of Einsiedeln.

Had Zwingli looked backward in some respects? Had he broken the cycle? Had the ancient propensity to killing been exorcised by his gospel? Which, wonders the pilgrim, was the greater event: the fracas between colliding Swiss cantons where Zwingli, intent on spreading the faith by force, had tragically fallen, or the dying to secular loyalties that occurred in the soul of Conrad Grebel? Which bespoke more clearly the nature of the Christ they both preached? Which was the greater release of spiritual energy? Which was truly new? Which brought the gospel of Christ into clearer confrontation with the structures of the world? Though there is no statue commemorating the second event, the pilgrim realizes that he bears its imprint in his own soul, after quiet centuries of preservation in the New World.

The growls of automobiles speeding along the Limmat and the sweep of their headlights bring the pilgrim out of his reverie. This is the industrial age, when the vanished guilds have been replaced by vast commercial combines, economic networks understandable only on abstract graphs. Many sons and daughters of many cities of this age feel oppressed and alienated, as Conrad tended to feel, and they look accusingly at the sword of authority in their government's hand, backed by business, as once here in Zurich the guilds elected the Council. Today, as then, the church still chaplains the wars, blessing and being blessed by the chambers of commerce. Many of these sons and daughters, like Conrad Grebel of Zurich, have run after momentary gratification, dreamed of glory, quarreled with their status-conscious parents, disappointed their teachers. Some will level off and join the responsible forces of their governments — their Zurichs.

Others, the pilgrim knows, will place all their youthful hopes in the kingdom of God, a new order of being for which the creation groans, and Caesar will summon them in vain to his bloody contests for political and commercial sway. For them, as for the Conrad in whose train they follow, all killing has been abandoned. They will learn, as he did, that in the crisscross of human loyalties there emerges a cross for those who break frontally with their earthly city, when it demands what their heavenly one denies. Jesus Christ is their Captain, and Conrad Grebel is their brother.

A final glance at the statue softens the pilgrim's heart. Without this mighty Ulrich, after all, could there have been a Conrad? What Christian has not come short of the loving nature of Christ, and how many of us have dreamed so great a dream as this preacher? This is the man whom Conrad, in the flush of his early faith, adored as "incorruptible." Yet he was drawn, by the logic of his loyalties, to that ancient jungle floor where human beings who have the option of being brothers in the family of God subject their destinies to the arbitration of tooth and claw.

And now for the airport at Kloten, close by the ancient monastery which once fed the Grebels' family coffers. Back to the New World, where Conrad's gospel, having slept in peaceful communities for nearly two centuries, has begun to awaken, and is challenged to further articulation by the sprawling in of the city. The pilgrim's fathers had eventually done what Conrad and his friends had joked about when fleeing Zurich's prison: they had gone to the red Indians over the ocean. These native Americans, like the pagan tribes of old, were detached from their patrimony with gold or alcohol offered by Christian hands, and driven off their lands by European weapons. And in large areas of that new country the Christian whiplash held sway for centuries over fields of dark human bodies kidnaped from Africa to work the Europeans' newfound soil.

The pilgrim senses, settling in cushioned comfort as his airship roars toward the stars, that for the past two centuries his quiet people have had surcease from the dreary slaughters of Europe, for that these sons of Conrad have only begun to engage their own Zurichs in living witness. Indeed, when their sons and daughters leave the green hills, or lately the suburbs and the cities, for the universities, they often carry with them no clear thought of the testimony Conrad purchased so dearly. As in Conrad's day, the media in whose sway they are formed are dominated by forces alien to the way of the cross, and they find it hard to conceive an alternative to the rule of these worldly powers — the kingdom of God.

So there is work to be done, a testimony to render, a story to be told. Perhaps it is good, muses the pilgrim as the Alps recede, that no statue of Conrad stands in his memory in the public square, since Conrad did not want anything to stand between Christ and His disciples. But there will be an imaginary seat in the circle for the outcast of Zurich when the pilgrim next breaks the bread and drinks from the cup in the fellowship of the church of Christ, in anticipation of a city wherein dwells righteousness, whose gates are never closed to its sons and daughters, and whose burgomaster is the Lamb of God.

The Author

John Landis Ruth, Harleysville, Pennsylvania, was born on a Mennonite farm halfway between Colonial schoolmaster Christopher Dock's home and the Salford Mennonite meetinghouse. He attended Lancaster Mennonite High School and Eastern Mennonite College, was ordained minister in the Franconia Mennonite Conference, and married Roma Jeanette Jacobs of Hollsopple, Pennsylvania. They have three children: Dawn, John Allan, and Philip.

The author majored in English at nearby Eastern Baptist College and at Harvard University, where he received his PhD in 1968. From 1962 to 1971 he served as pastor of the King of Prussia Mennonite Fellowship, which met in the Ruth home, and taught literature at Eastern Baptist College and the University of Hamburg in Germany.

He has written a drama, "Twilight Auction" (1966), texts for a cantata, "Christopher Dock" (1967), and an oratorio, "Martyrs' Mirror" (1971), both with composer Alice Parker, and has written and produced two films: "The Quiet in the Land" (1971) and "The Amish: A People of Preservation" (1975). His slide show, "Conrad Grebel, Son of Zurich," grew out of his book by the same title.

John continues to teach literature at Eastern College, and is currently supported in his writing and film-making by a group in Franconia Mennonite Conference. He serves on the boards of Christopher Dock High School and Mennonite Historians of Eastern Pennsylvania, and is associate pastor at the Salford Mennonite Church.

Colophon

The body type chosen for *Conrad Grebel, Son of Zurich* was Highland, a Photon typeface. The titles were created by Jan Gleysteen from a much-used antique Caslon foundry type, retouched where necessary, but retaining the charm of imperfection found in early printing. The text is printed in a brown-black ink on Origa offset paper. Throughout the first signature a sparing use of vermillion adds an accent reminiscent of Reformation era publications.

Conrad Grebel, Son of Zurich is bound in Skivertex Marbre which has the look of old leather. The jacket is printed in brown-black and vermillion on Sorg's Parchtex. All aspects of design, composition, printing, and finishing were done at Mennonite Publishing House, Scottdale, Pennsylvania.

The illustrations in this book are from the Anabaptist Heritage Collection gathered by Jan Gleysteen. The Swiss soldiers in battle and the Triumphal Entry of Christ are reproduced with the permission of the Kunstmuseum in Basel and the Landesmuseum in Zurich respectively. The other pictures were taken on location or in the historical libraries of Goshen College, Goshen, Indiana, and Eastern Mennonite College, Harrisonburg, Virginia.

The allegorical portrait of Grebel on the jacket is from a painting by the Mennonite artist, Oliver Wendell Schenk. It is one of three portraits representing Grebel, Manz, and Blaurock commissioned in 1971 by Laurelville Mennonite Church Center, Mt. Pleasant, Pennsylvania.

The endsheets feature an illustrated map of sixteenth-century Zurich carved in three joining wood engravings by Josen Murer and printed by Christopher Froschauer, the namesake nephew who took over his famous uncle's pioneer printshop.